More
FORGOTTEN
MURDERS
from Alaska

BETSY LONGENBAUGH

∿∿∿ Epicenter Press Inc.
Alaska Book Adventures™

KENMORE, WA

Epicenter Press Inc.
Alaska Book Adventures

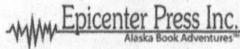

Published by Epicenter Press

Epicenter Press
6524 NE 181st St.
Suite 2
Kenmore, WA 98028

For more information go to:
www.Camelpress.com
www.Coffeetownpress.com
www.Epicenterpress.com

Author's website: full website TBA

Design by Rudy Ramos
The main street in early Tenakee Springs.
Alaska State Library Photo Collection ASL-PO1-4243

More Forgotten Murders from Alaska
2026 © Betsy Longenbaugh

ISBN: 9781684923342 (trade paper)
ISBN: 9781684923359 (ebook)

LOC: 2025949525

To my aunts Cathy and Sandy, who helped foster
my love of writing, history and a good story

Table of Contents

Foreword.. vii

Chapter 1:   A dead man in a bathrobe (Tenakee Springs)......1

Chapter 2:   The Birth of the Birdman (Juneau)......................18

Chapter 3:   Unserved Justice (Douglas) 32

Chapter 4:   Sinister Deaths in Petersburg (Petersburg).........44

Chapter 5:   Death of a Rum Runner (Juneau) 58

Chapter 6:   Groceries and a Gunny Sack (Ketchikan)...........75

Chapter 7:   The End of a Boy Hero (Juneau).........................93

Chapter 8:   The Cookie Jar Murder (Juneau) 108

Chapter 9:   The Fourth Husband (Juneau) 124

Chapter 10: Dismemberment in Sitka (Sitka) 135

Acknowledgments...152

Author Biography...154

FOREWORD
By Ed Schoenfeld

When Betsy started talking about researching historic murders in Alaska, I wasn't sure what to think.

We had both recently retired and were looking for something new, something different from our usual volunteer jobs. Food bank deliveries and cooking meals for our local homeless shelter were important, and so was helping out at church and repairing hiking trails.

But murder? Did I want us to become true-crime groupies who could tell you how many victims a particular serial killer had? What type of weapon they used? How arsenic kills a person, as opposed to cyanide? Whether bodies dumped in the frigid ocean waters of Alaska float or sink?

Still, Betsy's research plan promised depth beyond what we had written during our days as reporters. Getting today's story done and moving on to tomorrow's was fine as a job. But spending more time looking into the details of crime in our backyard was different. And I've always loved history.

The prospect of scrolling through century-old newspapers online and on microfilm was exciting. What knows what we'd find? Not just the details of long-ago killings, but an understanding of what our adopted hometown was like decades ago, and how people reacted in times of crisis.

Plus, the project gave us the chance to work together. We sat near each other at the same newspaper for three years in our thirties, but we co-wrote only one project and it was about sexually transmitted diseases. Not very romantic, was it?

So, we began our work, with the immediate goal of creating walking tours and museum presentations. That led Betsy to become an author, and this book is her third to be published.

I am amazed by what she can do. Betsy can just sit down and write. And write. And write. Whether fact, such as this book and its predecessor, or fiction, like her first novel, writer's block was not part of the equation.

While our tours and presentations have led us to be known locally as "The Murder Couple," it was clear that only one of us could be the writer. That was Betsy. I helped with research, editing and other tasks, but she had the clear vision of where a story should begin and end, and how facts should be presented in between.

Besides, I spent my pre-retirement year telling people I wasn't going to write a book. "What would it be about?" I'd asked. My life wasn't that interesting, despite four decades as a journalist. Plus, I didn't have the patience.

Betsy exceled at organizing the research, identifying crimes and checking though legal records, ranging from a few sheets of procedural court documents to reams of motions, rulings, testimony and jury instructions.

I was also having fun doing research, which often came with surprises. One of my first *WOW* moments was when I perused the file of a 70-year-old case involving the knifing of a popular store-owner. The sole evidence was a forged check, which helped convict and hang two men. Flipping through the court file, the actual check just sort of popped out. It was just sitting there, loose, amongst the other documents. This average-looking piece of paper led to the death of two of the very few African American men living in Juneau at the time. They were likely innocent.

Another time, I was looking into the background of a woman charged with murdering her husband by hitting him with a glass tumbler. I wondered whether she had been married before and whether any previous husband was still living.

I did some research and it turned out that the dead man was her fourth spouse. The license application for her second marriage listed her as a widow. And it looked like hubby No. 2 had also died. When I found out about her third husband and his untimely demise, I began to doubt her claims of self-defense. What a story!

Luckily, Betsy did more research and discovered that whole story of what is called in this book "The Fourth Husband."

I hope you enjoy "More Forgotten Murders from Alaska." If you haven't done so already, read its predecessor, "Forgotten Murders from Alaska's Capital," with a different set of cases. And I think you'll love "Death in the Underworld," Betsy's first novel. It's based on one of the most fascinating cases we've found.

There's also a fourth book, another novel, in the works. I've read parts, and it's good, but I can't wait to see how Betsy solves the crime.

—Ed Schoenfeld

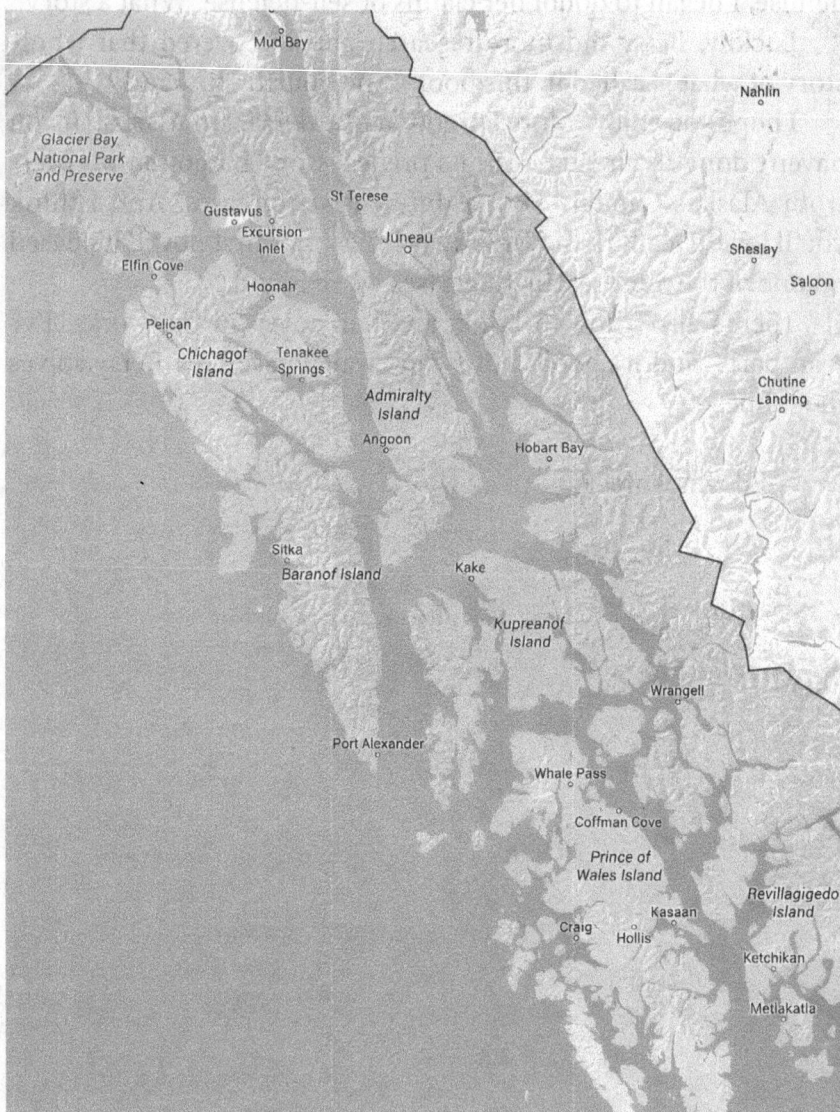

Map of Southeast Alaska

Chapter 1: A dead man in a bathrobe

It is easy to imagine the tiny town of Tenakee Springs, Alaska, as it was in 1906, when a "bad man" was shot to death in the town's general store. Tenakee Springs hasn't grown a great deal since that time – it remains a waterfront village without roads, sewer lines, or reliable cell service about fifty-six air miles from Juneau. The village's main draw is the same – the natural hot springs that gave the community its current name. It was likely the springs, as well as good fishing and a protected harbor, that drew Alaska's first people to the area. There is a bill of sale indicating that Ed Snyder, the white man who developed the area for other settlers, purchased the land, where he built his house and store, from Alaska Native Andrew Jack, who had a building on the property next to the springs.

According to the town's website, the word Tenakee is from the Tlingit word "tinaghu," meaning "Coppery Shield Bay." This refers to three copper shields, highly prized by the Tlingits, that were lost in a storm long ago.

In 1906, in addition to its springs, Tenakee had earned a reputation for being a safe place for bank robbers and other outlaws to hide, earning it the nickname "Robbers' Roost." Within relatively easy distance from Alaska's capital of Juneau, Tenakee's moderate climate, the absence of federal marshals, and the springs drew people on the lam from Alaska, as well as the Yukon, in Canada. The most notorious of these outlaws were members of Soapy Smith's gang, who ruled the gold rush town of Skagway through violence and other criminal behavior. Smith has been called the greatest grifter or scam artist in the West; he ran confidence games in Colorado and Alaska. His criminal colleagues are said to have

The main street, including Ed Snyder's store, in early Tenakee. *Alaska State Library Photo Collection ASL-PO1-4243*

settled in Tenakee after Smith's shootout death in 1899. An early account notes, "The town has several pool halls, bars and 'lots of gals.'"

It wasn't until 1917, when a notorious murderer was suspected of killing a local fisherman, that the community began seeing regular visits from a deputy federal marshal and a U.S. magistrate, called a commissioner at the time. But until then, the town was "wide open," encouraging the presence of prostitutes, gamblers, and others looking to make (or steal) a quick dollar.

While there was a seamier side of the community, Tenakee also drew people seeking health benefits from the springs. There are numerous mentions in early newspapers of men and women spending days or even weeks in Tenakee to recover from an injury or treat a chronic illness.

Just as in 1906, the public bath fed by the springs today is free and remains divided into men and women's bathing hours. (In those early days, women's hours were limited to six hours each day.) Those using the bath are required to be naked and to use soap and

Ed Snyder in his store, the site of the murder. *Photo courtesy of Tenakee Historical Collection.*

water to wash off before they enter. An unidentified author wrote in the May 15, 1912, edition of the *Douglas Island News* about his experience of a 1912 visit to Tenakee:

"The baths at Tenakee are simplicity simplified. You all bathe in the same tub or pool, which is a V-shaped gash in the solid bedrock, from the bottom of which bubbles constantly the mineralized water warmed in the bowels of the earth. The temperature of the water is about 105 degrees F, and as you enter the bathhouse you become conscious of deep heat, and a peculiar odor that makes you think of the doses of sulfur and molasses you took as a child. A feeling of depression comes over you and you begin to shed your duds, a process that you continue until you stand as nature left you, unadorned, ready for the plunge. It is hot at first, but you soon warm up to it, and are then ready for your blanket. Wrapping yourself from head to heels you lie down on a bench and the perspiration pours from you until you wonder if it is possible that you might just leak back into the pool."

Other than the blankets – likely a necessity without heating in the dressing room – the bath remains exactly as this visitor described. Today, just as then, the bathhouse is near the top of the main dock in Tenakee. Across the street lies the town's store, until recently named Snyder's Mercantile for Ed Snyder, who opened the business in 1898.

An early photograph of the Tenakee bath. *ASL P117-088 Alaska State Library Winter & Pond Photo Collection*

The *Mariechen* after her grounding. *P226-612 Alaska State Library*
William Norton Photo Collection

Although the murder happened in Tenakee, this story may have begun with a shipwreck almost twenty miles away. In 1905, a tramp steamer named the *Mariechen* was en route from Seattle to Vladivostok, Russia. The 381-foot-long steamer was transporting coal oil, meat, flour and other general merchandise, including beer. Carrying fifty crew members, the ship left Seattle on Nov. 19 and quickly ran into rough winter seas. Five weeks later, the ship was battling gale force winds that were continually driving waves over the deck.

On Christmas Day, a deadlight on the ship (a window of heavy glass, wood or metal that hinges inward) gave way. The engine room quickly flooded and the steamer's boiler fire was extinguished. Attempts to pump the water out failed, and the captain began a bucket brigade to carry it from the hold to the upper deck, where it was poured back into the sea. This onerous task removed enough water for the engineers to start fires in two of the upper boilers, providing enough power to allow the crew to steer.

The twenty-five-year old ship had been rigged for sails before being converted to steam, and the captain, Rudolph Heldt, put the crew to sewing makeshift sails in hopes of gaining some additional control in the rough seas. But the sails quickly blew away, the hand pumps became clogged, and the crew was again reduced to the bucket brigade. This effort continued for an exhausting thirty days – a period the captain called "one long battle for existence."

There was no telegraph or other method of communication aboard the *Mariechen* to seek help – such equipment wasn't required until the sinking of the *Titanic*, seven years later. Captain Heldt was unfamiliar with Alaska waters and found himself and the *Mariechen* in Chatham Strait, a 150-mile narrow passage between the mostly unoccupied islands of Admiralty and Chichagof in Southeast Alaska. In an account of the ship's travails, Tenakee historian Vicki Wisenbaugh later wrote:

"A northwest gale was blowing directly down the strait, and the ship could not proceed against it. It was three in the morning and snowing heavily. In desperation, Captain Heldt gave the order to turn the ship around. Swinging broadside in the gale, her bow was forced into the beach by the wind and sea, and she struck with a heavy crash."

The boat was grounded on Jan. 29, 1906, in False Bay, just eighteen miles from Tenakee. Two lifeboats were lowered, and everyone made it ashore. Some of the ship's cargo floated ashore and provisioned the crew as it waited four days for rescue by the passing steamer *Georgia*.

It didn't take long for nearby residents to discover the cargo from the now-deserted ship. Residents of the neighboring Native village of Killisnoo began collecting flour and other food. In Tenakee, residents likely focused less on flour and more on beer. It's the beer that may have led to the subsequent death of a Tenakee resident.

Norman E. Smith, a thirty-three-year-old who had recently opened a saloon in Tenakee Springs, saw an opportunity for cheap alcohol to stock his new business. Smith had already earned a reputation as someone who was willing to bend, break, and ignore the law, so when another Tenakee resident returned from the wreck with barrels of beer, Smith was quick to purchase them.

Smith was new to Tenakee. He opened his saloon and hotel near Snyder's Mercantile and appeared to be competing with Ed Snyder as the nascent community's leader. The two men clashed; seventy years later, old-timers in Tenakee remembered talk of Smith trying to kill Snyder. (These talebearers included Dermot O'Toole, Snyder's nephew and the owner of the store for many years.) According to their accounts, Smith fired a gun into the outhouse that Snyder was using. Apparently, Snyder leaned over (probably to reach for a catalog page to use as toilet paper), and the bullet went over his head.

Born in Maine, Smith had been in Alaska for some time before coming to Tenakee. He may have traveled north as part of the Klondike gold rush of 1886-89 but chose to make his home in Southeast Alaska. He was fond of cycling and may have built bicycles. In the census of 1900, he chose his occupation as cyclist, and a newspaper later noted he was well-known for bicycling. He was also an entrepreneur and a bit of a shady character. Old-timers remember him as someone who abused girlfriends. They also said he earned his nickname "Diamond" Smith after purportedly stealing a diamond-headed stickpin from a hunting companion. The stickpin's owner, according to Tenakee old-timers, did not return from the hunting trip.

In later courtroom testimony, a deputy federal marshal from Wrangell, about a hundred miles to the southeast of Tenakee, described Smith drawing a gun on him at a Juneau saloon. The bartender grabbed the gun from Smith before he fired it, but Marshal Grant believed he would have been killed without the bartender's rescue.

Smith was rumored to have property interests in several Southeast communities; the 1900 census shows the young man living alone in Fort Wrangel (now Wrangell). In 1905, he purchased all the stock and furniture from the Breedman's saloon in Douglas, Alaska. He also purchased three cottages behind the saloon. The saloon items, plus loans from Juneau businessmen, allowed him to open the Bay View Saloon and Hotel in Tenakee Springs. It's likely the three Douglas cottages were also moved to Tenakee; the house builders of the time were known for their tightly constructed buildings; a street in Sitka today includes several buildings that were taken apart and barged there from Douglas after its gold mines there closed.

The letterhead for Smith's Tenakee business advertised: "The Finest Wines, Liquor and Cigars – Domestic and Foreign." Smith went on to describe the Bay View thusly:

"A First Class Hotel has lately been established; fish and game served – both kept for guests – prices moderate. Hunting unexcelled. Bear and deer are plenty. Grouse, pheasant, geese and ducks in season. Climate mildest in Alaska, scenery grand, wide beach and no surf. Rooms, cottages and cabins for rent – everything furnished."

Another transplant to Alaska, Robert Reed, was spending winters in Tenakee; he worked there and elsewhere as a miner or trapper. A newspaper article later claimed he spent winters there for his health; it stated he had Bright's Disease, a term then used to describe chronic illness of the kidneys. Reed had moved to Alaska from California and, at thirty-seven, was five years older than Smith and single. He and Smith became friendly enough that he helped Smith build a cabin, although Reed later complained that Smith never paid him. At one point, Reed asked Smith to stay in his cabin and care for his dog during an absence. Reed returned to find that Smith had given the dog away. Whatever friendship they had was at an end, although they both remained in Tenakee.

After the tramp steamer Mariechen was wrecked, Reed was among the first to take his boat there. He returned to Tenakee with seven barrels of German beer and other pillaged stores. (The wreck could not be legally salvaged by anyone other than its owners because it and its cargo continued to be owned by the San Francisco businessmen who funded the delivery.)

In Tenakee, Smith promptly offered to buy the beer for $70. Reed agreed and returned to the wreck for more. While Reed was gone, Smith was asked about the beer by the local revenue collector, David Terwilliger. When Reed returned a month later, Smith demanded $150 to settle matters with Terwilliger. Reed and Smith negotiated that down to $37.50, but Reed asked Smith for a revenue license and receipt. Smith refused, and the dispute between the two men grew.

It wasn't until the fall, when Reed was again back in Tenakee, that matters came to a head. Reed later testified that Smith had come to his cabin on more than one occasion, threatening to kill him. He decided to remain in the cabin to avoid Smith and covered the windows so Smith couldn't see in.

Lee Pryor, a clerk at Snyder's Mercantile, later testified that Smith twice accused Pryor of ignoring him because Pryor was siding with Reed and had heard him threaten Reed's life on three occasions. Pryor said Smith came into the backroom of the store once when he was there and provoked an argument. Pryor said he saw what he thought was a revolver in Smith's pants leg, and it appeared to be falling to the floor. Pryor saw that Smith had his hand on another gun at his waist, and believed that if he, Pryor, reached down to pick up the falling gun, he would have been shot. He grabbed Smith's arm, and the two wrestled briefly before Ed Snyder came into the room and broke up the fight.

Snyder backed up Pryor's claims and said he had also argued with Smith, who once drew a gun while in the store. He also saw Smith hit a man in the store, knocking him down. Smith also visited Snyder's cabin in the middle of the night, looking for a woman with whom Smith had a relationship. This was the same woman another person later said had been whipped by Smith.

On Thursday, Nov. 2, 1906, Reed went to Snyder's Mercantile, where his friend Pryor was working. It's unknown what took him to the store, but Reed appeared to linger there for some time talking to an acquaintance.

On that same morning, Smith, who had been sick for the previous week, left his rooms above the Bay View Saloon wearing a duster over his bathrobe. He was accompanied by his friend, W. M. Deitrich, who said he knew Smith was unarmed because Smith's two guns were behind the bar in the saloon. Deitrich left him at the door of the store. Smith walked into the mercantile and asked Pryor for a particular size of stove pipe, which the clerk went into a storeroom to find.

When Smith entered the store, Reed was sitting at a table in the kitchen area at the back of the store talking with Claud Birmingham. Reed was facing the store's main door, and Birmingham had his back to it. Birmingham said he turned to talk to Smith and didn't notice Reed get up and walk into a back bedroom as Smith came over to the kitchen to talk to Birmingham. Birmingham said he asked Smith how he was feeling, and Smith replied, "not well."

Unknown to Smith, there was a loaded shotgun owned by Pryor that was resting against the wall in a back bedroom directly behind Reed. As Smith answered Birmingham's question, Reed slipped into that back bedroom, picked up the shotgun, pulled aside the curtain covering the backroom doorway and fired at Smith's head. Smith fell to the floor. A newspaper later described this shot as "blowing the top of his head off." Reed then walked into the kitchen from the back bedroom. Birmingham said Reed walked to Smith, leaned over his body and fired the second barrel of the shotgun, this time hitting his neck. Leaving the shotgun behind, Reed then left the store.

Deitrich later testified he saw Reed on the street outside the store, and Reed said to him, "I just killed your friend, Smith."

"What Smith?" responded Deitrich.

"Your friend, Norman Smith. I put two charges of buckshot under his hide."

Reed returned to his cabin and armed himself with a rifle and revolver before hiding in the nearby woods. Local resident C. A. Trundy was sent to put him in custody, and Reed surrendered once he was assured that other local residents weren't looking to avenge Smith. Reed was then taken to Hoonah to meet with the coroner's jury, a group of six men charged with determining a cause of death in suspicious deaths. The jury quickly decided that Smith was murdered, and Reed was the killer. Reed was returned to Tenakee, where the government convened a grand jury to consider the case. After the grand jury listened to several witnesses, it determined Smith had been killed by Reed. Reed was charged with first-degree murder and was sent to Juneau to await trial in jail.

Newspapers throughout Alaska printed articles about the shooting – most of them a paragraph noting that Robert Reed had killed "a bad man." The source of the articles was most often Juneau, where competing newspapers took opposing views on the case.

The *Daily Alaska Dispatch of Juneau*, which claimed to be the city's "official" newspaper, was quick to take sides. Its first article on the shooting claimed (falsely) that Reed was so frightened of Smith that he spent the previous three months sleeping at the mercantile. It also made some claims of earlier violence by Smith in Juneau, writing that Smith had attempted to pull a gun on a federal marshal in a Juneau saloon (true), and had grabbed the gun in the hand of a woman on a Juneau street as she shot at him (no corroboration). Given the name "Diamond Hattie," it is likely the thwarted shooter was a prostitute. (This mention later morphed into another Alaska newspaper claiming that Smith had "shot a woman of the half-world in Juneau.") The *Dispatch* article also made a point of calling Reed "a quiet and unassuming trapper."

The *Dispatch* continued to laud Reed after he arrived in the jail in Juneau. An article appeared at the top of the front page with the headline: "Reid Makes Favorable Impression at the Jail." A later piece noted that "It is the consensus of opinion that Reid should have a medal."

A competing Juneau weekly, the *Alaska Transcript*, wrote that other Juneau newspapers:

"seem extremely anxious to build up a public sentiment for the man who killed Norman E. Smith. The officer of the law who brought the prisoner from Tenakee spoke very highly of Mr. Smith and says he was "not the 'bad man' his enemies try to have it appear." The writer went on to say, however, that the same "officer of the law" spoke well of Mr. Reed.

In a later edition, the *Alaska Transcript* stated, "there is some evidence that goes to show there might have been a conspiracy formed to murder Smith." Again, there is no further mention of any conspiracy; it is likely the Transcript was trying to provoke its news competition.

Reed's defense was outlined in an affidavit he submitted to the court on Dec. 27, 1906, while awaiting trial in the jail in Juneau. The affidavit states he was frightened of Smith and had been warned about him by friends. Specifically, it states that one friend heard Smith say he went to Reed's cabin a few days before the shooting to kill Reed. Other friends, Alec and Mary Hart, told Reed the evening before the shooting they had heard that day that Smith was looking for Reed and planned to kill him.

Reed also named witnesses in the affidavit who would testify that Smith was a "violent, dangerous and turbulent man." Other witnesses would testify to Reed's good reputation, "peace and quietude."

The trial charging Reed with first-degree murder was, as was usual in those days, scheduled just a few weeks after the shooting – on Feb. 20, 1907, but it was delayed because the appointed judge, James Wickersham, was unavailable. The trial began in Juneau at the end of April, with a prolonged search for jurors. It wasn't unusual for it to be difficult to find jurors in Juneau – they had to be men, white and have no meaningful connection with the defendant or witnesses. That narrowed the pool from which qualified jurors could be selected for any trial. (Juneau had only about 1,800 residents then, and more than half did not meet the standards for court service.)

It took a day and a half before the panel was selected. Testimony began on Tuesday, April 30, 1907, and somewhat unusually, the judge chose to sequester the jury during the trial. This decision may have been due to the interest in the case by the local newspapers.

The defendant was represented by the law firm of Shackleford and Lyons of Juneau. The attorney appearing beside Reed in court was thirty-seven-year-old Thomas Lyons, who would go on to become a well-respected judge in the territory. The prosecutor was U.S. attorney John J. Boyce, who later left Alaska after being dismissed from his position by the governor in 1909.

The first day of the trial included opening statements from both the prosecution and defense, as well as testimony from three prosecution witnesses. The revenue collector, Terwilliger, testified about the conflict over the beer sale; Claud Birmingham described the shooting; and W.M. Deitrich described walking the unarmed Smith to the store. Deitrich also described hearing from the defendant after the shooting; "I put two charges of buckshot under his hide."

When the defense took over, Smith's attorney appears to have had a strategy that relied on many witnesses disparaging Smith. Thomas Lyons called nine witnesses on the day the prosecution rested, including both Lee Pryor and Ed Snyder. The following day, the defense called eight more before bringing Robert Reed to the stand. After his testimony, there were two more defense witnesses before the prosecution cross-examined three of the witnesses, including Pryor. The last witness of the day was Lucy Reed, Robert Reed's sister, who had traveled to Juneau from California to support her brother. Unfortunately, there is no description of her testimony.

The majority of the witnesses testified about their own encounters with Smith. Deputy Marshal Grant described Smith's attempt to shoot him in the Juneau saloon and said he considered him a "dangerous and violent man." Ed Oberman, a marine engineer and Tenakee resident, said he had seen Smith break one man's leg, whip a woman and knock down an old man. He said that Smith said he "owned all the deer around Tenakee and would not let any white man hunt them."

In a gutsy and what must have been an unexpected move, defense attorney Lyons asked U.S. attorney Boyce (the case's prosecutor) to the stand to testify about previous cases that he had heard against Smith. Boyce refused, "owing to his official position." The judge agreed to excuse him from testimony.

On the stand, Reed testified about Smith's threats against him, including the time Smith came to Reed's cabin with a gun and backed him against a wall, calling him "a vile name." The encounter was interrupted when a friend came by. Reed described hiding in the cabin and covering the windows after that encounter. He said Ed Snyder told him Smith came to the store, armed, looking to kill him. Alec and Mary Hart told the jury that they had warned Reed the day before the shooting that Smith was looking to kill him.

Reed described being at the store and talking to Birmingham when Smith came inside. The newspaper wrote: "Glancing through the door, he saw Smith with one hand resting on the lapel of his coat and the other reaching under his coat. He then was impressed that the hour had come." He said he took a hasty aim and shot. He said he intended to only shoot once and claimed the second shot was accidental.

Surprisingly, the prosecutor doesn't appear to have asked Reed whether the shooting was a setup. The sequence of events would suggest it may have been planned. Reed, a man so afraid that he covers his windows, hears from friends the day before the murder that Smith is out to kill him. The next day, he leaves the cabin where he's been hiding and sets himself up in the back corner of the only store in town, in a place where he can see anyone entering the building. While his friend talks to Smith, he ducks into a backroom, grabs a handy loaded shotgun and shoots Smith without a word to him (and without hearing a threat from Smith). It appears to have either been a deliberate setup or someone acting on intense fear. Both could certainly be the case.

The day ended, surprisingly, with prosecutor Boyce asking Judge Wickersham to allow Dr. H.L. Gillespie to examine Reed to determine his sanity. It is likely that this examination was a precaution on the part of the prosecution, since under the law, a person judged insane was not guilty. If it was, it was planned in advance, since Gillespie would have had to travel to Juneau from Oregon where he worked in an asylum, before the trial started. (It was noted in the newspaper coverage that Gillespie had attended the entire trial.) It is also likely that Boyce anticipated an insanity defense, since it had become known that Reed's mother was in an insane asylum.

After Gillespie's testimony, Boyce cross-examined Reed, but to no notable effect, at least according to newspaper accounts. Judge Wickersham then sent the case to the jury, after giving its members eighteen pages of instruction, including six possible verdicts: first-degree murder, first-degree murder without capital punishment, second-degree murder, manslaughter, not guilty and not guilty due to insanity.

In his instructions, the verbose Judge Wickersham told the jury to consider the claim of self-defense thusly:

"If you can find from the evidence in this case that threats were made by the deceased Norman E. Smith, to do the defendant great bodily harm or to kill him, and that such threats were communicated to the defendant prior to the killing and they and other facts known and appearing to the defendant, were such as to justify a reasonably prudent man in the belief which he was in danger from the deceased; then in addition thereto the defendant knew that the deceased was a turbulent and dangerous man, that he habitually carried firearms, and that the defendant believed he intended to kill him, then I instruct you the defendant was justified in acting in his self-defense on a hostile demonstration and of much less pronounced character than in such threats and other known facts had not preceded the killing."

In layman's terms, the judge said Reed did not need to be threatened with death in the moment but to have a belief his life was at risk.

The jury returned the following day, a Saturday, after meeting all night, with a verdict of not guilty. Apparently, the jurors believed that Reed had acted in self-defense.

Reed was freed from jail. According to historian Wisenbaugh, he returned to Tenakee just long enough to pack up his belongings and sell his cabin. He then apparently returned to California with his sister, Lucy Reed. He died in 1943 at the age of seventy-four in Stonyford, CA, with his only survivor his sister.

Norman Smith's remains were sent to Maine to rest with his family. According to a newspaper article in Maine, the family thought Norman had left an estate worth about $40,000, which in today's currency would be $1.3 million. It was enough to send both his father, Eugene, and his sister, Lydia, to Juneau. His father asked to be named administrator of the estate, but he was too late. Within a week of Smith's killing, Juneau businessman O.F. DesRocher petitioned the court to be appointed administrator, as did William Hanson of Tenakee. Both men were owed money by Smith. DesRocher was given the position. When Eugene Smith challenged the appointment, the victim's father was told by the court that he couldn't administer the estate because he wasn't an Alaska resident. Eugene responded by moving to Juneau and continued to raise questions about the estate's administration.

Not surprisingly, perhaps, Smith was found to have claimed ownership of some properties, including real estate and boats in Tenakee, that may not have belonged to him. The Bay View, however, was his, and the new administrator, DesRocher, promptly moved to Tenakee and reopened the business. He and three appointed appraisers inventoried Smith's Tenakee real estate, which totaled ten lots, four buildings, and a coal claim on Admiralty Island (DesRocher noted its value as worthless). In addition to real estate, there were "curios," according to the appraisers, as well as jewelry.

Among the jewelry was a diamond brooch. One of the estate's appraisers was Bert Wooldridge, formerly of Conrad, Yukon. Wooldridge and his wife were friends of a Miss Violet de Vere, who had lived in Conrad but was now living in Whitehorse, Yukon. The appraiser apparently told de Vere about the brooch. The Smith estate soon received a letter from de Vere saying that the brooch was hers and had been taken by Smith. "I hope there will be no trouble for the brooch certainly belongs to me," she wrote, following it up with an affidavit describing the brooch and invoice showing that she had paid $350 for it (more than $12,000 in today's dollars). After some gentlemanly threats by de Vere's attorney to the estate's attorney, the brooch was returned to Miss de Vere on Christmas Eve, 1906.

DesRocher continued running the Tenakee hotel and saloon, though there was a brief closure while he transferred the liquor license from Smith's name to his own, on the advice of the estate's attorney. In a May 1907 court report, DesRocher complained about continued interference from Smith's father, saying he had been "constantly harassed by letters, petitions and objection..." Smith's father did seem to have at least one valid concern. He pointed out that DesRocher had inventoried the contents of the upstairs safe at the Bay View without anyone else present. Perhaps that is where DesRocher found the unnamed "curios" he later took to Juneau to sell.

It's unknown how much of the estate eventually went to the Smith family; given Smith's debts, it may have been enough to pay for the family's travel to Alaska. DesRocher was called an "old-timer of Juneau and Tenakee" when the newspaper announced his death of heart failure just four years after he took over the estate. It doesn't say who inherited his estate.

The murder of Norman Smith continues to capture the imagination of longtime Tenakee residents. Vicki Wisenbaugh, who first researched this murder, began living in Tenakee in the 1980s and recalls Dorie O'Toole (a relative of Snyder's) showing Vicki the place on the floor of Snyder's Mercantile where Smith's body had fallen more than seventy years before.

Acknowledgement: Many thanks to Wisenbaugh, who shared her thorough research of this story with me and first brought it to my attention.

Chapter 2: The Birth of the Birdman

Robert Stroud was better known as the Peanut Kid when he and his older girlfriend, Mrs. Kate Delaney, stepped off a steamship in Juneau in 1908. They had traveled to the capital city from Cordova, Alaska, where Stroud had sold peanuts from a stand. The couple met in Cordova while Stroud was also making a hand-to-mouth existence fetching snacks and drinks for the "women of the underworld."

Mrs. Delaney was one of those women – a prostitute who was in her twenties by the time she met the teenage Stroud. A later, romanticized version of their meeting described the older woman tenderly nursing the teenager back to health after he was stricken with pneumonia. As with many of the often-retold myths of their time together, this story was likely the product of the imaginative biographer who wrote Stroud into national fame almost forty years later.

What is much more likely is that the couple saw in each other someone who could help them make a living – Mrs. Delaney by plying her trade and Stroud by finding clients and offering whatever protection an underweight, gangly eighteen-year-old could offer. It is to be hoped they also found some solace in each other's company; Stroud referred to Delaney as "my wife" in a letter to a friend, encouraging him, unsuccessfully, to join the couple in remote Alaska.

What Stroud lacked in physical strength, he likely made up for in street smarts. After all, he had been living off the streets for about three years after leaving his family home in Seattle. He traveled the rails around the United States, pimped for prostitutes

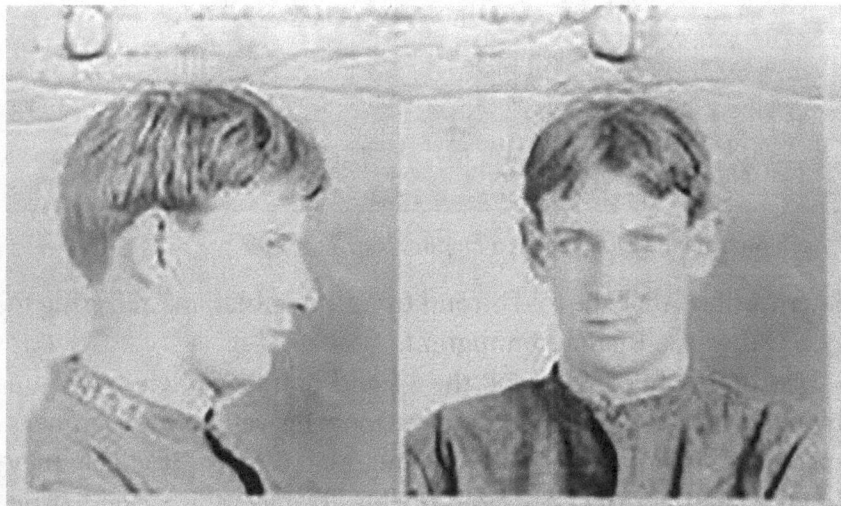

Robert Stroud as a young man.

on the docks of Seattle, and made his way to Cordova and nearby Katalla to work on a new railway.

When Stroud and Delaney arrived in the bustling capital city of Juneau, they faced some stiff competition. A 24/7 town with several active gold mines, Juneau and the nearby city of Douglas both had neighborhoods of what maps at the time delicately called "Female Boarding Houses." In Douglas, some forty prostitutes lived and worked in "the Restricted District" adjacent to downtown. In Juneau, a row of small houses, or prostitute "cribs," made up what was called The Line in the south of town. The newly arrived couple set up business in a room in the Clark Building in downtown Juneau. It appears Delaney practiced her trade at the residence of her customers, at least in one noteworthy case.

That case occurred on Monday, Jan. 18, 1909, when Delaney (whose street name was Kittie O'Brien) left the house of local bartender Charles von Dahmar after spending the night. The arrangement had been that von Dahmar would pay her $10 after entertaining him at what the newspaper called his "cottage" on Fourth Street downtown. Instead when she left at 5:00 a.m., he paid her $1. She took the dollar and returned to Stroud. Two witnesses

JUNEAU, ALASKA, THURSDAY, JANUARY, 21, 1909.

STRAUD AND KITTIE O'BRIEN HELD WITHOUT BAIL TO THE GRAND JURY—WOMAN NERVOUSLY FOLLOWS CASE—BOTH ARE CHARGED WITH MURDER IN THE FIRST DEGREE

Headline from the *Daily Alaska Empire*, Jan. 21, 1909

later testified that she told Stroud to "kill the Russian," referring to von Dahmer, a Russian immigrant.

Stroud obliged. He took the $1 and bought bullets for a gun owned by the couple. Later that afternoon, he went to von Dahmer's residence. Von Dahmer let the young man inside – it's likely they knew each other since Stroud probably arranged the earlier liaison with Delaney. Without warning, Stroud shot the bartender twice in the head. Stroud then stole whatever money he could find. The body was found with the pockets in its pants and jacket turned inside out. Stroud walked out the door of the house into the dark afternoon of a short winter's day.

He was met by the eyes of two men – a passerby and von Dahmer's next-door neighbor. Both men heard the shots, saw a man close the front window shade and watched the man's shadow bend over to go through von Dahmar's pockets. They asked Stroud what happened, and he replied, "Everything's fine," before quickly walking downhill to the bustling streets of downtown Juneau.

It may have occurred to Stroud that he was not going to get away with this killing. Just a few blocks away, he would have walked past the jewelry store of Emory Valentine, the owner of the Valentine Building and, at the time, Juneau's mayor. It may not have been too surprising that Juneau's police chief also happened to be in the store. Stroud likely recognized the police chief. He walked into the store and gave himself up.

The later myth about this murder – a fiction still appearing in contemporary accounts – is that Stroud found Delaney beaten and in tears after von Dahmer attacked her. Enraged by the abuse of his girlfriend, Stroud sought out the man, fought with him and accidentally discharged the gun. Overtaken with remorse, he promptly turned himself into the police.

In reality, the police chief took Stroud to the jail, which was in the bottom floor of the territorial courthouse. It was indicative of Stroud's state of poverty that he weighed in at less than 130 pounds, despite being six feet tall. His clothes were promptly taken from him and burned. The newspaper states that prison officials feared they were "full of vermin," most likely lice. He was also told to bathe before being dressed in prison garb.

Meanwhile, von Dahmer's next-door neighbor had fetched a federal marshal to the scene. Law enforcement found the dead man lying on the floor of his house, discovering no evidence of any struggle between the two men. The marshal and an enterprising newspaper reporter separately tracked down Delaney, who told both men that she had told Stroud to kill von Dahmer. Subsequent newspaper accounts don't note any other comments from Delaney. She wasn't reported to have said much more than "not guilty" in subsequent court proceedings.

Both Stroud and Delaney were promptly charged with first-degree murder. A Juneau newspaper of the time, the Daily Reporter, gave a lot of attention to the crime. It was sensational – involving a prostitute and a cold-blooded killing. It also hinted at a predatory older woman taking advantage of a younger man. The typical winter boredom of Alaska, as well as the death of a bartender (who was likely known by many of the town's residents) would have attracted a particularly attentive audience.

One article included a poignant description of Delaney the day after the murder. "Kittie O'Brien was very nervous and visibly ill at ease while in the courtroom. Her every act showed that she fully realized the terrible position she was in. The woman was clad in poor, cheap clothes, very much neglected and worse for wear. She is a faded blonde, potentially not over 30 years of age, but the lines of dissipation and care on her face make her appear considerably older. She likely never was an attractive looking woman. Her face is badly marred with sores at present."

While such a description answered the need to condemn a woman living on the fringes of society, it also answered two questions. Surely, if she had shown any evidence of a recent beating, it would have been noted in this description. And the facial sores may have helped explain the couple's poverty, since they could have indicated venereal disease to experienced clients. We know little more about Delaney, other than she had spent some years working as a prostitute in the Cordova area and had been the victim of a beating by a boyfriend some years earlier. It must have been savage since the boyfriend ended up serving time in jail for it at a time when violence against a wife or girlfriend was commonplace and generally unprosecuted.

Things were on track to move swiftly to a trial, conviction and sentencing – all for first-degree murder. There was the man who sold the bullets to Stroud, the witnesses who said Delaney told Stroud to kill von Dahmer, and the eyewitnesses to the murder. About six weeks after the shooting, the trial was scheduled.

But then, Stroud's mother, Elizabeth Stroud, appeared on the scene. Elizabeth Stroud had four children; two daughters from an earlier marriage, plus Robert and another son, Marcus, by her second husband. Stroud's two biographers have stated that the Stroud household was an unhappy one. Stroud's father was abusive, and his mother was manipulative, playing the children off each other and their father. It's not too surprising that Stroud left home when he was a teenager.

As soon as she received word of Stroud's arrest, Elizabeth Stroud left her home in Seattle and steamed north, accompanied by a lawyer. Although she and her estranged husband were not well-to-do, Elizabeth's father had been. A midwestern judge, he was reputed to have left an estate worth about $1 million when he died in 1908. It's perhaps not surprising that, shortly after his death, Elizabeth had the money to secure a divorce and move to Juneau with a lawyer.

The lawyer quickly put a cog in the wheels of justice. Arguing that the Daily Reporter's extensive coverage of the case would disallow an impartial jury to be chosen in Juneau, he sought a change of venue to Valdez, Alaska. Today that may seem like an odd request – Valdez is more than four hundred miles away from Juneau and a relatively small community. At the time, however, it was the center of several mining concerns and a thriving town with an active court. It was not unusual for judges and prosecutors to serve both Valdez and Juneau.

The court agreed to a change in venue but moved the trial to nearby Skagway instead of Valdez, and set the date for June, giving the defense more time to prepare. And, as it turns out, it was more time to arrange a plea agreement. The trial date passed by without notice, but in August, there was a court hearing. Stroud agreed to plead guilty to manslaughter.

It was a gift to the young man, who turned nineteen while in the Juneau jail. If convicted of first-degree murder, he would either have been hanged or sentenced to life in jail. It may also have been a gift to his mother since Elizabeth Stroud made a point of attending all court appearances, sitting next to her son and holding his hand. The newspaper noted she also made a point of glaring at Delaney, who was being represented by Stroud's attorney and would have stood trial by his side.

The judge sentenced Stroud to 12 years – at a time when a manslaughter conviction in federal court led to sentences of between 1 and 20 years. Delaney was released. It would have been impossible to prosecute her for murder when the person who shot the gun pled out to manslaughter, which means accidental death. She disappeared into the shroud of history; research doesn't reveal a death or burial site.

Stroud was sent to McNeil Island, the federal penitentiary on an island near Seattle. His mother and younger brother, Marcus, settled down to a new home in Juneau. Marcus later wrote about being a local paper boy.

The McNeil penitentiary has been compared to Alcatraz; it was situated on an island and had earned its own notoriety as a tough place to serve time. Stroud would have recognized the type of people who populated the jail – they were the same sort of men he had been hanging out with in boxcars, wharves, and shady locations for the past few years. It was a grim, old building that had been first used as a military prison. Stroud later wrote, "(It) fell upon my spirits and reduced them to the lowest point in my experience. … I was frightfully lonely, frightfully miserable."

Just two years after he entered the penitentiary, Stroud had an argument with a fellow prisoner that ended when he used a homemade shiv (knife) to stab the other convict in the back seven times. The man didn't die, but Stroud ended up handcuffed to the bars of his cell for four months and had six months added to his sentence. This relatively light additional sentence was as much a reflection on how officials viewed the injury of prisoners in their care as on their opinion of Stroud.

A year later, the young man was transferred to the new federal penitentiary in Leavenworth, Kansas. Construction had just ended when Stroud entered it. Leavenworth was one of three federal penitentiaries at the time, including McNeil and a prison in Atlanta. Leavenworth was the largest of the three and was built as a maximum-security prison. Although new, it was still a prison, and its occupants suffered, especially during the hot summer months, when the concrete structure radiated heat with little ventilation.

In Leavenworth, Stroud threw himself into what was to become a life-long interest in continuing education. For most of his life, Stroud claimed he left school after the third grade, but this just likely fed another life-long interest – inflating his ego. By saying he left school after third grade, his academic achievements as an adult appeared more impressive; his mother, however, said he left school after the seventh grade. Regardless, he took advantage of any education he could find in prison, studying mathematics, science, and literature. He also became a Theosophist, a member of what has been called a religious cult that connected a higher power to a divine wisdom, a belief that fed his sense of superiority.

He took up painting and decorated card stock, which he sent to his mother to sell. Despite enjoying learning, Stroud maintained a poor attitude in jail and continued to get in trouble with authorities.

In 1916, six years before he would have been released from jail, Stroud killed a prison guard during mealtime at Leavenworth. He stabbed the man, Andrew Turner, with another homemade shiv, killing him instantly in front of hundreds of people. In a chilling letter to his father, Stroud later wrote, "The guard took sick and died all of a sudden. He died of heart trouble. I guess you would call it a puncture of the heart. Anyway, there was a knife hole there."

Andrew Turner, the prison guard killed by Robert Stroud, photographed at his wedding.

His motive for the killing is unclear, but biographers have suggested that Stroud was angry with the guard for denying a recent visit by his brother. The killing took place before the entire prison population and Stroud quickly stood trial for first-degree murder. His mother, Elizabeth, again rode to his defense and moved from Juneau to Kansas City, where the trial was held. She sold her Seattle house and some land she owned and hired an attorney. At the trial, she instructed the lawyer to enter pleas of self-defense and insanity on Stroud's behalf.

Stroud objected, claiming he was in his right mind when he killed the guard. But on the witness stand, his lawyer had Stroud justify the murder through his belief in Theosophy. Completely unrepentant, Stroud spoke of reincarnation, his belief in his own personal moral code and how the killing was inspired by a higher being he called "The Master."

While the testimony may have sounded like that of a madman, the strategy didn't work. Stroud was convicted and sentenced to hang. But his lawyer successfully appealed based on problematic jury instructions. Stroud was retried and convicted again in 1917 – without the insanity defense. This time, he was sentenced to life in prison. He appealed that conviction too, though his lawyer advised against it. Federal officials didn't object, hoping a third trial would bring another conviction *and* a death sentence. The third trial achieved the prosecutor's aims, and Stroud was again sentenced to hang.

This was unusual for Kansas. No one had been hanged in that state since 1870 - almost a half-century before. The state banned capital punishment in 1907 (it was reinstated in 1935), but the murder charge was filed in federal court, and the killing was on federal property. So, gallows were built, and the hanging was scheduled.

Once again, Elizabeth Stroud came to the rescue. She began a petition drive to seek commutation of the sentence to life imprisonment and succeeded in gathering signatures from Juneau residents, as well as Kansans who opposed the death penalty. She took the petition to the president of the United States, the only person with the power to commute the federal sentence. President Woodrow Wilson was incapacitated; he had suffered a stroke in 1919, and his wife had (unofficially) taken over his duties. Wilson's wife agreed to the commutation, despite the protests of the Attorney General of the United States, and just weeks from being hanged, Stroud escaped death.

Prison officials were unhappy and decided that while they had to house Stroud, they would do it on their own terms. They decided his time would be spent in solitary confinement. In the 1994 book *"The Many Faces of Robert Stroud"* by Jolene Babyak, the author suggests Stroud's avowed homosexuality may have played a role in this decision. Babyak, whose father worked at Alcatraz prison, wrote that openly gay prisoners were viewed as especially dangerous by prison authorities because it was believed they would aggravate feuds and jealousies, causing unrest and violence. Homosexuality was also considered "deviant" behavior and defined as such by mental health professionals until 1973.

So Stroud was placed in solitary, where he continued his studies but also developed some new interests. He began researching birds. His interest was apparently sparked by finding an injured sparrow in the prison yard. He took it inside to care for it and then began learning about and caring for canaries kept by other prisoners.

It's difficult to overstate the importance of canaries to Americans of the time. They were among the most popular household pets in the 1920s, in large part because of their singing. Orchestras and bands of the time performed with singing canaries, and owners were known to carry the birds' cages from room to room, the way later generations would carry a portable radio.

But the bird owners had little recourse if their singing friend became ill. Veterinarians back then cared exclusively for commercial animals, such as cows, horses, and sheep. An ill pet might be treated with household remedies but was typically expected to either die or get better on its own.

Canaries were so ubiquitous that they had even made their way into prison cells during this period of the early 1920s. There were no prison rules forbidding pets in the cells and officials may have welcomed the birds' calming influence. But, just as occurred outside the prison, a sick bird had little or no informed care. Other prisoners began giving their sick birds to Stroud, who used them to continue his ornithological studies.

It would be easy to see Stroud as a man whose impulses had led to his imprisonment and whose soft side was now being exposed through his care and nurturing of these little birds. That image was at the core of the popular *Birdman of Alcatraz* book and ensuing movie, starring Burt Lancaster, which purported to be about Stroud.

It is not, however, the truth. While Stroud reveled in teaching his pet birds to perform tricks for the prison warden and visitors, he was coldly unsentimental about them. He even went so far to suggest to bird owners that they dissect their diseased companions using the same tool he did – his fingernails.

In addition to studying the birds' illnesses, Stroud began breeding and selling canaries, using his mother, who took orders and helped mail birds, as his business partner. He regularly wrote for ornithological magazines and earned a reputation among bird fanciers even before his book, *Diseases of Canaries*, was published in 1933. His fellow bird enthusiasts did not initially know Stroud was a prison inmate.

Diseases of Canaries was a very popular book since it finally gave Americans a guide to caring for their singing companions. It was, however, heavily reliant on another ornithological book of the time (uncredited by Stroud). It also contained "treatments" that were essentially worthless.

Meanwhile, Leavenworth officials were getting increasingly impatient with Stroud. Initially, when national magazines and major newspapers began writing about the inmate who had redeemed himself through self-study, prison officials were happy to include a stop at Stroud's cell on any tour by notable visitors. But despite accommodations to Stroud to allow him to continue his breeding business, including giving him a second, adjoining cell and laboratory equipment, the prisoner continued to demand more privileges and showed no gratitude for what he had already received. He was also becoming an increasing drain on prison resources. For example, prison policy required all incoming and outgoing correspondence to be retyped by administrative staff for security reasons. Stroud's copious correspondence would have been a massive job, possibly requiring one staff person dedicated just to his communications.

Stroud relied upon his mother for advocacy and help with his business for years, but in 1929, at the age of thirty-nine, he began corresponding with Della Mae Jones, a forty-eight-year-old widow from Indiana. They didn't meet in person for three years, but they ended up marrying (involving another concession to Stroud's demands by prison officials), and Jones took over from Elizabeth Stroud as the prisoner's business partner. The new relationship caused an estrangement between mother and son that appears to have been unresolved when Elizabeth died in 1936.

In 1942, conflicts with prison officials came to a head. The prison was losing staff members to World War II enlistments, and Stroud

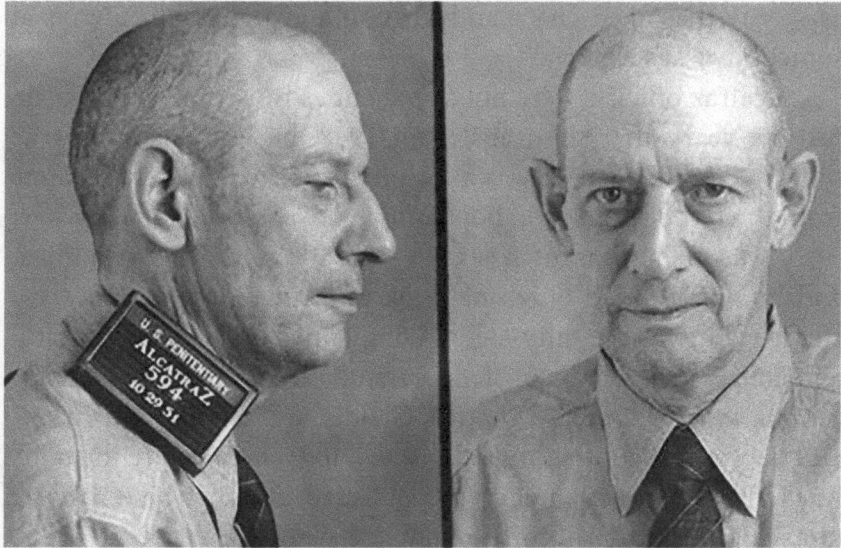

Robert Stroud as an older man

was continuing his unceasing demands for more accommodations (he also began what became a life-long refrain of refusing parole unless it would be given with absolutely no restrictions). Two guards arrived at Stroud's cell and told him he was leaving right then for Alcatraz Federal Penitentiary, off San Francisco.

Alcatraz was considered the prison for the worst of the worst. This decision by Leavenworth officials must have felt fully justified when a search of Stroud's now-vacant cells found an alcohol still that included light bulbs used as flasks and several containers of alcohol. They also found, according to author Babyak, that Stroud had "carefully hollowed out a niche under one of the tables and put a stiletto-like dagger in it, so arranged that it could be taken out and used instantly."

Stroud was initially placed in a wing at Alcatraz dedicated to its more troublesome prisoners, who weren't allowed to mingle (or eat with) the general population. He was also denied his birds, so he instead began studying languages. He became known as an agitator who enjoyed stirring up trouble, leading in one case to a mini-riot described by Babyak. A fellow inmate described him as "a guy that liked chaos and turmoil and upheaval... always at somebody else's expense."

Alcatraz officials were not as patient as those in Leavenworth. Just six years after the transfer, in 1948, he was placed in true solitary confinement. It was a hospital room completely separate from the rest of the prison population.

It was not a pleasant existence – the room didn't have a toilet, and he was allowed only one book at a time. He continued his studies, but at age fifty-eight, complained of several physical ailments and had bouts of depression. It didn't help that *The Birdman of Alcatraz*, by Thomas Gaddis, was published in 1956, and he was not allowed to either speak to Gaddis before the book was written or read it after it was published, although he was aware of its publication from correspondence.

Perhaps because he lacked the chance to speak to Stroud, Gaddis's book was a romanticized version of the real story. It began with the book's title, which may sound more interesting than the "The Birdman of Leavenworth" but is factually incorrect, since Stroud never had a bird in Alcatraz. Gaddis went on to portray Stroud as a victim, first of Kitty's so-called abuser and then of a power-hungry guard. Apparently, without any attempt to verify them, Gaddis accepted all of Stroud's claims to earlier reporters about his intellect, bird studies and general academic superiority, including some outright lies about having a college degree and receiving other accolades.

Given what Stroud had to have known was a fawning biography, it must have been even more upsetting when he wasn't allowed to read it or be interviewed by the many writers who wanted to talk to him after the book's publication.

The knowledge that the book was there and was becoming a best-seller may have led to Stroud twice attempting suicide, acts that finally prompted Alcatraz officials to transfer him to the federal hospital prison in Springfield, MO in 1959. Stroud, now sixty-nine, wrote of his happiness there – finally able to walk outside and be with others. In fact, officials noted, his being with others included being discovered naked and in the act of intercourse with a younger man.

Although Stroud was happier in Springfield, it is likely that the officials there were just as aggravated as those in earlier prisons. When the film, *The Birdman of Alcatraz* was released in 1962, they refused to let Stroud view it. Burt Lancaster, who portrayed Stroud in the film, created such a sympathetic character that one former inmate who knew Stroud expressed outrage about the actor's depiction.

Stroud died in Springfield in 1963, at the age of seventy-three; a photograph of his gravesite at one time showed several people had left toy canaries there. He remains one of the best-known prisoners who served time at Alcatraz.

Chapter 3: Unserved Justice

It was the closed curtains that worried Fannie Miller. Her close friend, Babe Brown, would always let the light in when she got up in the morning. That was the signal that Babe was ready to have coffee with her neighbor in the Restricted District.

The date was Dec. 13, 1916, and Babe Brown and Fannie Miller were prostitutes who plied their trade in the area that was intended to contain the brothels and cribs of the Douglas underworld. The two women had their own cabins on First Street in the Restricted District. The street paralleled the Douglas Island beach, was a few short blocks from the downtown district, and ended with a dairy barn and a rocky beach. The fact that the street was a dead end would have contributed to its use as a containment area for prostitutes. Only men seeking their companionship (and the carpenters working in the nearby shop) would have any reason to be on the street. It also made it simple for respectable women of Douglas to ignore its inhabitants.

Founded in 1881, Douglas was primarily intended to serve the neighboring town of Treadwell, where the largest gold-producing mine in the world operated during the early 1900s. The company town offered housing, a swimming pool, a library and schools to its workers. But if the mine workers wanted a beer, church service, or an evening with a woman of the underworld, they had to travel about half a mile to downtown Douglas.

Between downtown Douglas and Treadwell was the Indian Village, a neighborhood where all Alaska Natives and their families were forced to live. Although there were boarding houses and single-family homes in Treadwell, the company town, Alaska

Photo of Douglas First Street in 1908. Further past it, to the left, was the Restricted District, where prostitutes worked and lived. P226-291 Alaska State Library William Norton Photo Collection

Native workers were not allowed to live there. Douglas housed a hospital operated by the Catholic Sisters of St. Ann as well as a private hospital operated by a Dr. Weyerhauser. Other businesses included multiple saloons, shooting galleries, grocers, cigar stores (most likely brothels), and even a candy factory.

In December 1916, Douglas was only a few months away from the April 1917 collapse of the mining tunnels that ran under the Treadwell mining complex. The result was a quick end to three of the four gold mines on Douglas Island and an exodus from Treadwell and Douglas. That was still in the future on this winter morning.

Fannie became increasingly concerned about her friend as the curtains of her small cabin remained stubbornly closed, and there was no response to knocks or calling out. At about 1:00 p.m., she finally flagged down a passerby. The man obligingly forced open the door to the cabin, which contained two rooms – a front room

THE ALASKA DAILY EMPIRE

"ALL THE NEWS ALL THE TIME"

VOL IX, NO. 1267   JUNEAU ALASKA, WEDNESDAY, DECEMBER 13, 1916   PRICE TEN CENTS

GREAT BRITAIN CONSIDERS PEACE PROPOSALS
DOUGLAS WOMAN IS MURDERED

Banner headline in the *Alaska Daily Empire* on Dec. 14, 1916, the day after the killing

Secondary headline in the *Alaska Daily Empire* on Dec. 14, 1916, the day after the killing.

PITIFUL HISTORY OF WOMAN VICTIM, FORMERLY OF ANCHORAGE, WHO MET BRUTAL DEATH RECENTLY AT DOUGLAS

and a bedroom behind it. Fannie Miller stepped past him to enter the bedroom. The newspaper reported:

"On opening the bedroom door, she gave a loud scream of murder, for the bed, floor and walls were spattered with blood." The newspaper went on to note that she "found the body partly wrapped in a blanket, the head being crushed on each temple with a blunt instrument, a knife wound leading from the bridge of the nose to the brain and the throat badly cut."

Douglas was without its own police force or federal marshals, so the coroner, John Henson, came to the scene of the crime and summoned marshals from Juneau, the town across Gastineau Channel. As the Territorial Capital, Juneau also housed the head of the federal marshal program for the territory as well as its own police force. The deputy federal marshals would have arrived via the ferries that regularly plied the waters of the channel, traveling from Juneau and the town of Thane on the mainland to the communities of Douglas and Treadwell on Douglas Island.

The newspaper said investigators found a new machinist's hammer behind a dresser and bloody water in a wash basin with a blood-stained towel next to it; apparently where the killer had cleaned up.

The cabin had been searched, and the investigators soon discovered that Babe Brown had been robbed. She reportedly had more than $3,000 in cash and jewelry. It appeared the killer was familiar with where Babe kept her purse because it was found in a trunk in her bedroom with the bottom sliced open and emptied.

The trunk also contained letters from its owner, revealing her name was not Babe Brown but probably Jennie Lind, Kline, or Poplasky. Documents in the trunk revealed that she was from Russia and was Polish and Jewish. In 1916, the country now known as Poland had already been annexed by several other countries, including Russia.

Investigators quickly began talking to possible witnesses. One neighbor told officers she saw a tall man with a soft fedora hat pulled over his face enter the cabin used by Jennie (Babe) around 3:00 or 4:00 a.m. Another witness saw such a man on the ferry the night of the murder. At 9:00 a.m., a carpenter employed at the nearby shop saw footsteps in fresh snow leading from the cabin. He guessed the prints came from size 8 shoes; the prints were melted by the time investigators arrived at the scene.

The coroners' jury met at the cabin within a few hours to look over the scene and talk to witnesses the marshals found. The jury consisted of six white men who were paid a stipend to determine the cause of death in the case of any suspicious death. The jurors quickly concluded this death was a murder caused by an unknown man.

Among the witnesses the jurors interviewed was Fannie Miller, who, despite her concern about her friend, appeared to know very little about Jennie. Most surprisingly, she claimed to know nothing of a man named Againsky, who other women of the neighborhood said had recently appeared in Douglas, claiming to be Jennie's husband. Fannie did reveal, however, that her real name was Ester

Segall; she was also Jewish. It was common practice then, and still is today, for prostitutes to assume aliases when working.

The murder, certainly one of the most brutal in the history of the area, drew a lot of attention and a lot of investigators. In addition to Juneau Deputy Marshals James Manning and Frank Back, Juneau city officer William Shaffer was involved. The day after the killing, P.J. McGuire was asked to join the investigation. P.J. was a detective now living in Juneau who had earned his fame seventeen years before with his involvement in solving three murders in the Yukon.

Phillip Ralph "P.J." McGuire was born in Pennsylvania in 1869, the seventh of eleven children. He left there in 1889 and by 1895 was in Minnesota, married and working as a detective. On February 15, 1900, he introduced himself to the Northwest Royal Mounted Police (NWMP) as a detective hired by the family of one of the three men who disappeared on a trail in the Yukon on Christmas Day, 1899.

Working with Constable Alick Pennycuick of the NWMP, McGuire conducted an amazing feat of detective work. McGuire used his dog to find the site of the murders, off a trail near the Yukon River. P.J. and Pennycuick then spent six weeks examining the site, sifting through dirt and digging into snow to find the pools of blood marking where the men died, as well as gun cartridges and some of the dead men's belongings. They determined where the bodies had likely entered the river. (All three were found down river after the spring thaw.) A man named George O'Brien was arrested after he was found to have a big dog that had belonged to one of the victims. A second man also believed to be involved in the killings was never seen again, but O'Brien was convicted and hanged.

Both Pennycuick and McGuire became well-known detectives after that case. It is unknown what brought McGuire to Douglas to help with this new case. It is unlikely there was a monetary motive since there is no one who would have paid for him to help solve the crime. At the time, the newspapers lauded his involvement, certain he would find the killer.

But the Juneau investigators were convinced they already had their man. The man who readily admitted that Jennie was his wife, Harry Againsky, matched the witnesses' descriptions of the man on the ferry and the man who entered the murdered woman's cabin the night of her death. The newspaper described him thusly: "The husband was described as a man about six feet tall, inclined to stoop and weighing about 170 pounds; so dark complexioned and with such kinky black hair that he might easily be taken for a dark Slav or Mulatto."

Againsky, according to witnesses, lived in San Francisco but had traveled to Anchorage to

DEPUTY MANNING ARRESTS MAN ON JUNEAU STREET

Suspect Taken to Jail on Warrant Sworn Out by Deputy Working on the Case.

MURDER, JURY VERDICT

Conflicting Statements Are made at the Inquest Held Yesterday at Douglas.

Againsky arrested headline in *Alaska Daily Empire* on Dec. 16, 1916, two days after the killing.

fetch his wife. According to the Daily Alaska Dispatch, his steamship was unable to dock in Anchorage once it arrived. Passengers who were taking that ship south were ferried to the boat. Among those passengers were Jennie and her friend, Fannie Miller. They were planning to leave Anchorage to escape Againsky, who they feared was en route. Since Againsky hadn't yet disembarked, Jennie must have been shocked to find him aboard the boat on which she planned to leave. Having accomplished his task of finding Jennie, Againsky didn't disembark, remaining aboard with the two women for the trip south. The ship left Anchorage on Sept. 25, 1916.

The ship stopped in Juneau, where Againsky, Jennie, and Fannie got off. The two women quickly set up business in Douglas. Againsky initially worked at the Treadwell mines in Douglas but was fired "on account of being of a most disagreeable temperament, and it was thought not feasible to have him working underground." He was fired on December 9, four days before the killing.

At the time of the murder, Againsky was living in Juneau in a boarding house near the dock where the ferry that ran between Douglas and Juneau landed.

Witnesses said that Jennie wanted to leave her husband; one witness said "she had no use for her husband and had tried to 'shake' him." The attempt was unsuccessful. When searching Jennie's cabin after the murder, Againsky's watch and chain and his bank book were found in her trunk.

On Friday, December 15, three days after the murder, Againsky was arrested. With Againsky behind bars, the public waited for the next step, not knowing the investigators were completely thwarted. A week after the murder, Againsky brought forward an alibi witness. The night of the murder, he said he was sharing a bed with a local barber, who provided the alibi. (In those days, some boarding houses had "shared beds" that made an overnight stay cheaper and gave more profit to the boarding house.) Againsky had also hired an attorney as soon as he learned that he was to be questioned, which investigators viewed as suspicious.

Investigators became angry with Ester Segall (the real name of Jennie's friend Fannie Miller), who had told the coroner's jury on the day of the murder that she didn't know of Againsky's existence. By this time, the investigators knew that was a lie since it was common knowledge in the Restricted District that Jennie's husband was in Juneau. They arrested the young woman and charged her with perjury. Segall was then placed in a jail cell near Againsky in the bottom floor of the territorial court house. A newspaper said that investigators believed she could be the key to solving the case.

While the marshals kept Againsky in jail despite his alibi, they continued trying to break the case. Among the evidence found in the cabin was a bloody handprint on the wall above the wash basin half-filled with bloody water. One of the local newspapers asked why investigators weren't looking at fingerprints, a relatively new forensic science. It had begun being used in court in the United States in 1912 but doesn't appear to have been considered by the marshals or the detective in this case, which is unfortunate, because it's likely that Againsky's alibi would have fallen apart in the face of such evidence.

Againsky was almost certainly the killer. In addition to not looking for fingerprints, the four investigators didn't think to question prostitutes in Anchorage. A couple of weeks after the murder, an enterprising reporter in Anchorage talked to some of Jennie's friends there, and the Anchorage newspaper introduced a completely new angle to the murder.

BLOODY CRIME AT DOUGLAS IS BEING PROBED

Assassin Is Believed to Have Committed Deed When Excited to a Frenzy.

INQUEST BEING HELD

Coroner's Jury Will Be Investigator of All Rumors Regarding the Murder.

Headline from the *Anchorage Daily Times* describing Babe Brown's history, Jan. 11, 1917.

The friends described what Jennie had told them about her past and her present. They said Jennie had been a victim of what we would now call an international sex-trafficking cartel. The Anchorage newspaper described it as "one of the most notorious white slave gangs now operating on the Pacific coast." Jennie told her fellow prostitutes of being wooed at her home in Russia by a young Jewish man who described himself as a wealthy American. His name was Againsky. Although she was only thirteen, her parents agreed to his request to marry her. They had a wedding ceremony before he was to return to America (he did not tell the family it was not the United States, but South America). On the ship to America, she was joined by another girl, who Againsky had also supposedly married. The ship landed in Buenos Aires, Argentina, and both girls were forced into prostitution.

This Anchorage news story may initially appear to be an attempt to sensationalize an already sensational murder. However, contemporary research and reporting document the existence of a sex trafficking cartel operated in Buenos Aires from the 1860s to the beginning of World War II. Initially called the Warsaw Club, the ring's members preyed on Jewish girls. The girls often came from homes where antisemitism had already impoverished families throughout Eastern Europe. When a prosperous-appearing young Jewish man came courting their daughters, their parents were usually happy to see their daughters enter what promised to be a secure marriage.

Once the ship landed in Buenos Aires, however, the girls found they were surrounded by officials who had been bribed to ensure they remained prostitutes. The conspiracy Jennie was now part of included bribed immigration officials, police, and judges, all of whom contacted the so-called husbands if the girls sought police aid. The girls could be beaten and sent to a lower class of brothels if they tried to seek help.

The cabal was sophisticated enough, according to *Bodies and Souls* by Isabel Vincent (2006), that it hired other men to write letters back to the homes of the (usually illiterate) girls, enclosing some money and laudatory comments about their wonderful lives in America. The result, of course, is that among the Jewish population in Europe, no families were alerted that their daughters were being forced into prostitution. Vincent, who won a Canadian National Jewish Book Award for her book, described one woman who wrote the truth to her parents. Her letter, however, was quickly followed by a missive from her so-called husband stating that his wife had been seduced by another man and had become a prostitute. The parents then cut their daughter off.

The *Anchorage Daily Times'* reporter described Jennie as one of these girls. The newspaper account said her friends said the woman, known in Anchorage as "Portuguese Jennie," told them she had given birth at fourteen. Vincent's book said it was common practice for the men to impregnate their abductees quickly to tie them even closer to the men. The babies themselves, however, were taken away and never seen again. Jennie had also told them that Againsky beat and whipped her.

The article mentioned that when Againsky first brought Jennie to San Francisco, police there identified her as a possible witness against the Warsaw Club. They arrested her but she served ten months in jail "rather than divulge any of the secrets of the well-organized gang." Jennie's friends told the reporter that she spoke several languages but was illiterate when she arrived in Anchorage. She became acquainted with the other women after asking them to teach her how to read and write. Consequently, she began writing to her family back in Russia. Their return correspondence was found in her possessions in Douglas, revealing her true name.

Friends told the Anchorage reporter that Jennie "was adept in fine needlework" and described her thusly: "She was perfectly molded... especially good natured and free hearted, she made many friends among the girls, to whom she confided that she had thrown away her wedding ring and would never go back nor send them any more money."

Convinced that Jennie was loyal to him, probably because of the San Francisco imprisonment, Againsky had sent her to Anchorage without him. She was expected, however, to send him the money she made. As Jennie grew in confidence, she strained at her ties to Againsky.

Her plan was to leave Anchorage for Cordova, where a railroad was being built and there would have been lots of business for the young woman. The Anchorage Daily Times wrote, however, that as she was headed onto the southbound steamship, her so-called husband grabbed her. He had apparently become suspicious when she stopped sending money and traveled to Anchorage to confront her.

However informative this personal history might have been, word of Jennie's past didn't make it to the Juneau investigators.

It appears that the investigators were still hoping for enough evidence to convict Againsky because on Jan. 23, 1917, he was indicted by a grand jury for murder. By April, however, the investigators realized that the alibi witness had stymied them. Instead of charging Againsky with murder, the U.S. District Attorney decided to seek another indictment. The grand jury obligingly indicted Againsky with six counts of violating the Mann Act, formerly named the "White Slave Traffic Act." The Act made it a felony to engage in interstate or foreign commerce transport of "any woman or girl for the purpose of prostitution or debauchery, or for any other immoral purpose."

Somewhat surprisingly, Againsky pled guilty to this and was sentenced to one year and one day in a federal penitentiary by Judge Robert W. Jennings. He was sent to McNeil Island Penitentiary outside Seattle. There are no records indicating where he went once the sentence ended.

The judge did not grant him time served in sentencing him. Againsky was in the Juneau jail from Dec. 15, 1916, until he was sent to McNeil in May. His sentence didn't formally begin until June 1, 1917, so he spent six months in jail before his sentence began. Draft registration records indicated that he registered for the draft while at McNeil; the United States entered WWI in 1917. His registration card states that his permanent address was in San Francisco.

Againsky was also held in Juneau for five months so he could testify against his attorney, Alexander C. Young. Young had recommended that Againsky plead guilty. Young was subsequently brought before the Juneau judge for disbarment proceedings in April 1915. Againsky had accused Young of defrauding him of all his money. Againsky testified that he paid Young $1,350, but had received an accounting for only $650. He also said that, after convicted, Young visited Againsky in the jail and told him that all of Againsky's money would be seized by the government, so he should give it to Young for "safe keeping." Againsky gave him a check for the remainder of his funds but did not receive a receipt.

The court took the $589 that Young said he still had of Againsky's money and returned it to Againsky.

Interestingly, Ester Segall ("Fannie"), who had been charged with perjury in this murder case, had also hired Young as her attorney. During the disbarment hearing, she said she had paid him $150, but he didn't even come to court for her and refused to refund her. She ended up pleading guilty, but the plea was set aside due to her lack of representation. She consequently hired two more lawyers for $200, who represented her when she pleaded not guilty. She was found not guilty.

As a result of the April hearing, Young was permanently disbarred from practicing in Alaska. Judge Jennings noted that Young's Alaska disbarment joined the disbarments he had already received from New York and New Jersey. When all the trials were over but Againsky was still in the Juneau prison, the Juneau newspaper reported that Jennie's body was shipped to San Francisco at Againsky's expense. It is unknown what happened to her body from that point onwards.

Chapter 4: Sinister Deaths in Petersburg

At 11:45 a.m. on a Wednesday, May 21, 1919, Ah Lee, a Chinese employee of the salmon cannery in Petersburg, Alaska walked over to the residence of the cannery's manager, Mar Kim.

It was part of Lee's job to deliver lunch to Mrs. Kim at her home every working day. Fung She Kim lived there with her husband, their young daughter and their eight-month-old son. Lee enjoyed the company of the three-year-old girl, May Wen Kim, and on that fateful day, he left a little early so May Wen could walk with him to the cookhouse to pick up the meal.

The house was near the cannery, next to the largest bunk house that boarded the many workers who toiled at the Petersburg Packing Company during the busy fishing season.

Ah Lee let himself into the house and went into the kitchen. There, he found the bodies of Fung She and May Wen, lying in a pool of blood and hacked to death with a bloody axe lying on the floor. The Petersburg Commissioner, the first official at the scene, described how the crime scene began on the front steps of the house, where he found bits of bone. A bloody trail led into the house and along the hall into the kitchen. The outside kitchen door was locked, with the key on the inside of the lock. A newspaper account later stated that the faces of both mother and child had been particularly attacked. The infant boy in the family was apparently in a bedroom elsewhere in the house. He was physically unharmed.

After finding the bodies, Lee ran to the cannery to tell Mr. Kim, and the authorities were notified.

Another witness told authorities when the victims were last known to be alive. Ye Bond lived above the Kims' home and said he was making coffee there when he heard Mrs. Kim and her daughter talking. He testified that he left the home shortly afterward at 10:20 a.m. According to the *Ketchikan Chronicle*, that testimony provided Mr. Kim with an alibi, since he was known to be in his office between 10:20 and noon.

WOMAN AND HER BABE MURDERED IN PETERSBURG

Mrs. Mark Kim, Wife of a Chinese Foreman, and a 3-Year-old Baby Killed With Hand Axe

The headline that appeared in the *Alaska Daily Empire* on May 22, 1919, the day after the bodies of Fung She Kim and her daughter, May Wen Kim, were found.

Petersburg has been known for its rich fishing grounds since before recorded history. Tlingit hunters and fishermen used the surrounding area at least 2,000 years ago. At low tide, the remains of their ancient fish traps and petroglyphs can still be seen. Alaska Natives still comprise more than ten percent of the population, and a federally recognized tribe is located in the community. Tlingits knew the area, which they used primarily as a fish camp, as S'eet Ka'. Today, a pair of totem poles at the corner of Petersburg's Haugen and Nordic Drives tell the story of the Tlingit ancestors traveling down the nearby Stikine River to settle and live in the area.

In 1897, Norwegian pioneer Peter Buschmann arrived. Seeing that the nearby LeConte Glacier could provide ice year-round for preserving fish, he built the Icy Strait Packing Company cannery, a sawmill, and a dock. His family's homesteads grew into the town of Petersburg, populated largely by people of Scandinavian descent. By 1920, 600 people lived there year-round. In 1920, its population had grown to more than 850.

To this day, the little town still retains its original Norwegian flavor. Each winter, local businesses host "julebukking," a tradition of offering refreshments and drinks to shoppers the week before

The Pacific Coast and Norway Packing Cannery, which became
the Petersburg Packing Co., where the victims and killer lived. P01-
4243 Alaska State Library Photo Collection

Christmas. Its community hall was built by the Sons of Norway
in 1912 and still hosts events year-round. And in May, the Little
Norway Festival celebrates Norwegian Constitution Day, which
brings many visitors to the picturesque fishing town.

Back in 1919, Petersburg was one of more than thirty
communities throughout Southeast Alaska that were part of
what was sometimes referred to as the second "gold rush," when
the growth of salmon canneries followed the coast from the
Columbia River in Washington state up into Southeast Alaska.
The first industrial fish cannery was established in California in
1864. Within two years, the owners decided to move it north to the
Columbia River, where they worked with local Native Americans
to fish for the salmon and brought in Chinese workers willing to
accept the lower wages offered for cannery work.

This pattern of seeking cannery workers from Asia and Pacific
Island communities would continue for decades, although the
fishermen, especially in Alaska, tended to be non-Native (many
were Scandinavian or Italian) by the time this murder occurred.

Salmon canning had replaced salting fish as a preferred preservation method, and canned salmon became a staple of many American kitchens, with most of the fish coming from North Pacific waters, especially Alaska.

Cannery workers came from China, the Philippines, Japan, and other Pacific countries. Although Chinese immigrants made up just .002% of the American population at the time, they were viewed as taking jobs away from white people, so in 1882 Congress passed the Exclusion Act, which was buttressed by the Geary Act of 1892, making Chinese immigration illegal.

Many of the Chinese cannery workers who had immigrated prior to 1882 were considered especially valuable due to their skills and training. Cannery owners often relied on that expertise to train new workers. These experienced workers continued to be active in Alaska canneries for many years after new Chinese immigrants were outlawed.

The sentiments that led to the Exclusion Act had also led some Alaska communities to force their Chinese populations out. In Juneau, for example, anyone identified as Chinese was forced aboard a boat by miners at the neighboring Treadwell Gold Mine and sent away from town in 1886. Only one Chinese man was allowed to remain, a local business owner known as China Joe, who was famous for providing flour to the town's occupants during a particularly harsh winter. The 1920 census indicates that only fifty-three Chinese people lived in the entire state of Alaska.

Mar Kim was one of them. Kim's arrival in the United States from China is not recorded in newspapers of the time, but he registered for the World War I draft in 1917, noting his age as twenty-nine and that he had a wife and child who were solely dependent upon him.

May Wen Kim's birth occurred in Seattle in October of 1916; her father Mar Kim, whose occupation then was noted as "merchant" on the birth certificate, was twenty-eight years old. Her mother Fung She Kim was just nineteen. By the following year, when Mar

Kim registered for the draft in July, he noted that his occupation was "cannery foreman" for the Petersburg Packing Company. Two years later, the Cordova newspaper wrote that "Petersburg claims to be the birthplace of the first Chinese baby born in Alaska. It arrived last week at the home of Mar Kim, foreman of the Petersburg cannery, and is a boy."

Although most Chinese were not welcome in Alaska (or elsewhere in the country) there were a few exceptions. Like China Joe in Juneau, Petersburg embraced a Chinese business owner, Sing Lee. Lee was a merchant and boarding house owner, as well as a noted philanthropist, donating, among many gifts, funds to build a new floor for the local basketball court. In 1932, at the age of eighty, he was also the victim of a murder, although no one was ever arrested. His body was found beaten in his store. It's interesting to note that he was an attendee at China Joe's funeral when the Juneau businessman died in 1917.

May Wen Kim's birth certificate; she was the first child of Mar and Fung She Kim, and age four when she was killed.

It is likely that Mar Kim had been chosen to be the foreman at the Petersburg Packing Company because he was Chinese, since the workers were primarily Asian. It was a responsible position and indicative of the owners' confidence in Kim's abilities.

Despite the horror of a crime that included the vicious killing of a child, news coverage was not as sensational as other murders that occurred in the same period, most likely because the victims were not white. The Petersburg newspaper, a weekly publication, offered only the initial story of the crime, the arrest of a suspect, and then reprinted one lengthy article from the subsequent trial in Ketchikan, about 110 miles away.

Although Petersburg is located almost equidistant between Ketchikan to the south and Juneau to the north, it has been traditionally more connected to Ketchikan, probably because both cities' economies were based on fishing, while Juneau historically relied on gold mining. In 1919, Ketchikan was home to both a federal courthouse and a daily newspaper.

Trial coverage may have also been affected by the shooting death of a deputy federal prosecutor, Steve Regan, who was killed on a Ketchikan street by Patrick Shannahan in October 1919, as the Kim trial was occurring, also in Ketchikan. This story featured the death of a federal official, as well as the death of a white man, so it consumed much of the Ketchikan news coverage of the time.

The initial article in the Petersburg newspaper noted that the murder did not appear to be motivated by theft, since rings, a locket and other jewelry on Mrs. Kim were untouched. It also commented on Mr. Kim's reaction, saying he was "heartbroken and... unable to account for the deed because he did not know that either he or his wife had an enemy in the world." It went on to state that, "There has been no troubles between the men and their boss this summer."

At the time of the murder, the deputy marshal assigned to Peterburg was in Juneau. The initial investigation was left in the hands of Petersburg Commissioner M.S. Perkins. In those early territorial days, a commissioner acted in some degree as a federal magistrate would today. He had authority to levy fines, write summons and warrants in legal manners, and could hear minor legal issues. He was also the coroner and was expected to view any suspicious deaths before the bodies were moved.

Despite the absence of the federal official who should have headed up any murder investigation, Perkins acted swiftly. He called a coroner's jury to the scene. He also arrested and charged a cannery worker with murder on the same day the bodies were discovered.

Japanese immigrant Mirato Mikami, thirty, was seen standing outside the Kim house by the same witness, Ye Bond, who testified that he heard the victims talking when he left the house at 10:20 a.m. Other cannery workers told investigators that Mikami was missing from work during the time of the murders and that he had changed clothes and shoes during his absence.

Mikami had arrived in the United States at age sixteen, sailing from Japan to Honolulu and then making his way east. According to passenger records in 1905, he arrived in Honolulu knowing how to read and write (unusual among his fellow passengers), listed his occupation as laborer and had $8.50 in cash. Those records stated he apparently came from Japan without any other family members. He never married, according to his registration for the draft and later documents.

The "evidence" that seemed to capture the imagination of the newspapers of the time, however, was an investigator's decision that the killings must have been done by someone who was left-handed. The prosecutor initially claimed that there was only one left-handed man in Petersburg, and he was Mikami. Another account changes that claim to "only one left-handed worker at the cannery." Both claims are unlikely, since current estimates are that 10% of the world's population is left-handed. The 1920 census shows a population in Petersburg and immediate surrounding areas of 879. That would mean about eighty-seven people in the community were likely to have been left-handed.

Although there are memorable examples of left-handedness being key to finding a killer or attacker, these are generally attached to fictional stories, not actual crimes. The idea appears in *To Kill a Mockingbird*, when the defendant's crippled left hand is used by his attorney as evidence that he couldn't have committed the attack with which he accused. In one case of an actual crime, investigators determined that London's Jack the Ripper, who killed women in 1888, was left-handed. It is now thought that this determination may have led these historical investigators to miss possible suspects. It is now common knowledge that it is difficult, if not impossible, to claim a wound is inflicted by a left hand, since attackers may use a non-dominant hand or strike from an angle that appears to be coming from the left, but isn't.

There are also some inherent prejudices and misunderstandings that may have guided this now-disproven theory. Left handedness is associated with evil, even with the devil; the word sinister means "from the left-handed side." In the United States, it was only in relatively recent times that children weren't punished if they were left-handed – forced to learn to write with the right hand or taught to write in an awkward position that mimicked a right-handed slant to their cursive handwriting.

According to a 2013 article in the *Smithsonian Magazine*, left-handed people continue to be distrusted and disliked in two-thirds of the world. In China, for example, only 1% of the population is identified as being left-handed, although there's nothing to support the notion that Chinese people inherently have a much smaller left-handed population. And in the Muslim tradition, the left hand is considered "dirty," and it's offensive to offer that hand to another person, even in assistance.

In 1919, however, the prosecutor seized on the defendant's left-handedness as damning evidence. He went as far as to use dolls to act out the attack during the trial, presumably proving the attack could have only been done by someone who was left-handed. The *Ketchikan Chronicle* described the scene in the courtroom:

"Attorney Charles Cosgrove [the prosecutor] had two large dolls in the courtroom and drew an imaginary picture of the room where the murder was committed, using the dolls to represent the victims of the tragedy. Mr. Cosgrove advanced a theory which would explain all the circumstances in the case as shown by the evidence. ...

He used the two dolls, showed the jury how the blows which killed the victims could only have [been] delivered by a left-handed man, how a right-handed person could not possibly have inflicted the cuts on the bodies, and then proceeded to attempt to prove to the jury from the evidence as it had been introduced, that the defendant is a left-handed man and the only left-handed man who was in Petersburg at the time the crime was committed."

He went on to describe the motive behind the killings as driven by "animal passion," saying the defendant had an unrequited love for Mrs. Kim.

The trial where this scene was acted out began on Wednesday, Oct. 29, 1919, in Ketchikan. After seating the jury, both the defense attorneys and prosecutor appear to have foregone opening statements. Instead, prosecutor Cosgrove put his first witness on the stand. C.O. Parks of Petersburg was called to testify as to the geography of the cannery, specifically the distances between buildings. His testimony was buttressed by maps of the area. Parks was a Petersburg businessman; some years after this testimony, he became business manager of Petersburg's weekly newspaper. It is unclear why he was considered an expert witness on this topic.

The second witness was Ah Lee, the Chinese cannery worker who discovered the bodies. He described going to the Kim's house at 11:45 a.m. to pick up May Wen so she could accompany him to the cookhouse to collect the family's lunches. Instead, he found the bodies.

The next witness was Mar Kim, the cannery foreman who had lost his wife and child. According to the Ketchikan newspaper, he "told of his family life" and also testified that he had seen the defendant, Murato Mikami, "pay attention" to Mrs. Kim. The newspaper account concluded, with frustrating vagueness, that he also testified "of many minor details which tended to connect Mikami with the dead."

The final witness on this first full day of the trial was Petersburg Commissioner M.S. Perkins, who described seeing the crime scene after being alerted of the murders. He also described the coroner's inquest, during which Mikami refused to interpret for the other Japanese workers, despite his having better English than his co-workers.

During the coroner's inquest, there was also testimony that the jury members examined the hands of all the cannery workers. Perkins said that, of the entire cannery crew, only three workers had clean hands: two workers who were ill and confined to their beds and the defendant. In another newspaper account, Perkins testified of "damaging admissions made by the defendant" during conversations with Perkins and four other men, including the doctor who examined the bodies.

It was testimony from Dr. C.H. Upton that the jury heard first on the second day of the trial. Upton described the condition of the bodies when he examined them. He also testified that "the wounds could only have been delivered by some person holding the axe in his left hand and illustrated why this was the case."

Perhaps the most damning evidence, absent the left-handedness of the defendant, came from two of his fellow cannery workers, Angel Delecerna and Uehara (the Japanese roommate of the accused, who was only ever identified by one name). They testified that they were "trucking tin" from the dock warehouse to the cannery warehouse with the defendant during the morning of the murders. (This likely refers to the metal that formed the cans used in processing.)

Uehara said that, "Mikami disappeared from the work shortly before 10 o'clock on the morning of the murder and... he was absent until nearly 12 o'clock." He testified that Mikami wore a pair of yellow shoes in the morning before he left his co-workers. Uehara then identified those as being the same shoes entered into evidence by the prosecution.

Uehara said that when Mikami rejoined the workers, he was wearing a pair of black shoes. He also testified that the defendant "was pale and frightened and that his face had a greenish, sickly look."

During what the reporter called "a vigorous cross examination" by the defendant's attorneys, Will H. Winston and Henry Roden, Uehara stuck to his story about the shoes. He said he remembered the change in footwear so clearly because when he tossed a box to Mikami early in the day, the defendant told him not to mar his shoes, which Uehara noted were yellow. Later, after Mikami returned from his absence, the defendant dropped a box of tin and cut the cap off his shoes, which were "old black shoes."

Both the coworkers said they were sure that Mikami had been gone from 10:20 a.m. to about 11:30 a.m., because he returned to work in time to haul only one load before the arrival of the steamship *Admiral Nicholson*, which docked at 11:45 a.m.

A third witness, another cannery worker, also testified that he noticed Mikami being absent from work "shortly after 10" and didn't see him again until shortly before noon. He said that the defendant then "looked sick and nervous and... threw himself down on the dock in the sun." He had also noticed the change in shoes.

During the remainder of this fifth day of the trial, several witnesses testified that they had seen Mikami walking toward the Kim house. The most important witness may have been Ye Bong, who lived above the Kim residence. His testimony helped set the time of the murders since he said he heard both victims shortly before he left his rooms at 10:20. He also said he had seen Mikami "standing near the rear corner of the house, looking toward the door to Mar Kim's rooms and acting in a suspicious manner."

In another abbreviated statement, the newspaper noted that the prosecution had shown "clothing, consisting of underwear, which was found hidden in the woods near the hog pen, belonged to Mikami." It also referred to the prosecution showing that Mikami "was in the habit of making advances to family women" without any additional description of testimony to that effect.

Wednesday, Nov. 5 was the sixth day of the trial, and apparently the prosecution had rested. The only defense witness that was put forward was the defendant, Murato Mikami. He spent all morning testifying and enduring cross examination. He challenged the testimony of coworkers Delecerna and Uehara, saying he worked with the two men until about 10 a.m., when he took a break of about 10 minutes to "watch some men catch fish." He denied having changed shoes and said he did not wear the yellow shoes, which were found in his possession blood stained. He did admit that the shoes were his.

The afternoon was taken up with closing arguments. The prosecutor took the occasion, as described above, to use dolls and a drawing of the room to "prove" that the crime had been done by a left-handed man and that Mikami was the only left-handed man in Petersburg. He also reminded the jury of the testimony by Mikami's coworkers of his changing clothes and shoes, his absence from work and his being seen near the house where the Kims resided. Although Assistant District Attorney Cosgrove gave most of the closing argument, it was concluded by the Federal District Attorney for Judicial District One (Southeast Alaska), James Smiser.

Defense attorneys Henry Roden and Will Winston then took turns giving the closing arguments for Mikami. The men were a somewhat odd pair – they had evidently been appointed by the judge to represent the defendant and it's likely the judge was putting a less experienced lawyer under the tutelage of someone with more expertise. Roden was a Juneau attorney and Swiss immigrant who had been practicing law for some time and was forty-six at the time of this trial. Winston, on the other hand, was just twenty-three years old (one wonders if he had taken the bar without attending law school – not uncommon in those days).

Winston spent most of his argument making a case against accepting only circumstantial evidence in a murder conviction. He noted that the prosecution had never recovered bloody outer garments, just the under clothes. He also ridiculed the idea of the attack being traced to a left-handed person. He even showed the jury a piece of wood he said he chopped during the lunch break and asked the jury members to determine which of his hands wielded the axe.

Despite his past legal experience, Roden opened with what must be considered one of the weakest closing arguments ever given. He began by saying he had been convinced of the guilt of his defendant until he heard all the evidence. The newspaper wrote that he then, "concluded that he was not convinced of the guilt of his client."

Roden then went over the timeline established by witnesses in detail. He said that it would have been impossible for the defendant to commit the crime in that period of time, change clothes and return to work.

After hearing these arguments and then receiving instructions from Judge R.W. Jennings, the jury left to begin deliberations at 9:40 p.m., according to court records.

In his instructions, Judge Jennings told the ten jury members they had several options when considering a verdict. They could convict Mikami of first-degree murder with capital punishment, first-degree murder with a sentence of life in prison, first-degree murder of only one of the victims, or acquit him of all crimes. It's unknown why he didn't describe other possible verdicts, including second-degree murder and manslaughter.

It took the jury just three and a half hours to reach a verdict, returning to the court at 1:10 a.m. with a unanimous decision to convict Mikami on both counts of first-degree murder. Somewhat surprisingly, the jury also decided the penalty should be life in prison, not the death penalty. That is likely because circumstantial evidence was (and still is) considered to be weaker than more convincing evidence, such as an eyewitness to the crime.

The Ketchikan newspaper reported that Mikami "sat like a stone image" until the verdict was read, when "a slight paling of his face was the only evidence showing that Mikami heard or was interested in the verdict in any way."

Murato Mikami, who was thirty at the time of the murder, appears to have spent the rest of his life at McNeil Island Federal Penitentiary, located on an island near Seattle, Washington. At McNeil, he appears in census records through 1940, when he was

```
3451- MURATO MIKAMI
Murder 1st.Degree without Cap.Punish.
Convicted Ketchikan,Alaska,11/7/19
Sentenced November 12,1919 to  LIFE
Received at Prison November 18th.1919
Sentence begins November 18th.1919.
 " Expires with G.T. NATURAL LIFE
Arrested Petersburg,Alaska May 22,1919
In Jail from Arrest.
Age  30  years,  Height 5'  8"
Weight 105¼# Net.  Hair Black.
Brown Eyes,  Japanese.
TEETH: All intact.
Scalp Numerously scared by Alopecia.
```

Murato Mikami's prison card after his arrival at McNeil Island Federal Penitentiary in Washington

fifty-one years old. He doesn't appear in the 1950 census records. His grave may be among the 125 unmarked headstones in the McNeil Island graveyard. The federal prison was closed in 1986.

Mar Kim remained in Petersburg for some time but continued to claim Seattle as his main residence. In 1924, the *Seattle Star* noted that he was to be the manager of a new Chinese opera house, which opened in Seattle's Chinatown in July. The article referred to Kim as "one of Chinatown's leading citizens."

Kim remarried and ended up living to age fifty-nine, when he died while traveling to Manila with his wife, whose name is not provided in the news article about his death. The article notes that he had been a grocer in recent years and left six sons and three daughters. It appears that he was not buried in Seattle, although his first wife and eldest child are.

May Wen Kim and her mother, Fung She Kim, rest next to each other in the Mount Pleasant Cemetery in Seattle's Queen Anne neighborhood.

Chapter 5: Death of a Rum Runner

It was the evening of July 4th, 1923, when an acquaintance beckoned William Lott into a Juneau restaurant, Harry's Grill. There, the affable barber walked over to a group around a man named Billy Prentice. It was 10:00 p.m. but not yet dark on this summer night in Southeast Alaska. Lott, a fifty-seven-year-old Black man, joined Prentice and his seven acquaintances in the small downtown restaurant. Within minutes, Prentice, a thirty-six-year-old White man who was a well-known bootlegger, was lying on the restaurant floor with four bullet wounds. William Lott was back outside, surrendering to a police officer who had responded to the gunshots.

It took Billy Prentice three days to die from his wounds, and the local newspaper said he believed during most of that time that he would recover. But he understood just before he died that it was the end and reportedly said, "The jig is up," as his last words.

At his request, he had also dictated a statement that William Lott had been the man who shot him. He didn't say why Lott did it in his statement and he didn't sign it. In court later, the defense and prosecution argued about why he didn't sign the statement. The prosecution said he couldn't sign because of his wounds. The defense attorney said he chose not to sign. The judge decided to let the statement be read to the jury.

It didn't really explain much – the jury had already heard from a number of witnesses that Lott was the shooter. Before the trial would end, Lott himself admitted to killing Prentice.

The question was why.

Prentice was not well-liked in Juneau. He was not only a

Photo of Harry's Grill from the court documents on this case. *Courtesy of Alaska State Archives.*

bootlegger but well known for his battles with police. During arrests both in Cordova and Juneau, he had resisted enough that police needed to use billy clubs and fists to handcuff him.

Despite numerous arrests for bootlegging and what appeared to be plenty of evidence, charges against him were always dropped, or he was acquitted. Witnesses left town or refused to testify, and charges seemed to evaporate. At the time of his death, he had spent time in jail but not for any significant charge.

Billy Prentice moved to the Juneau area about sixteen years before the shooting. His first job was as a pipe fitter for the Treadwell gold mine complex, located next to Douglas, across Gastineau Channel from Juneau. His first legal charge related to illicit alcohol appears to have been in 1914 when he was arrested while bartending at a Juneau saloon that was illegally open on a Sunday. He was probably working there part-time, since he was also employed at the Treadwell Mines but obviously took his work to heart. The newspaper reported that he had assaulted the officers who arrested him and "used obscene language." He was fined $100, and the saloon owner was also arrested for "profaning the Sabbath."

At the time, Treadwell was coming to the end of its highly successful life as one of the largest gold mines in the world. In 1917, just a few years after Prentice began working there, most of the complex closed after a tunnel collapsed, allowing ocean water to flood three of the four mines. The timing was perfect for Prentice to begin his next career as a bootlegger.

A year after the mines collapsed, the Alaska Territorial Legislature passed the Alaska Bone Dry Act, a voter-approved law banning the sale and transportation of alcohol. Alaska's prohibition was a precursor of national prohibition, which began two years later in January 1920.

In Alaska, as elsewhere in the nation, prohibition was tied closely to the suffrage movement, seeking to give women the right to vote. When Alaska became a territory in 1913, the first act of the Territorial Legislature was to grant that voting right to Alaska women. Women were a crucial force driving prohibition. Women's groups had identified alcohol as a chief ingredient in the disintegration of the American family and were avid supporters of prohibition. World War I also played a role, with supporters of dry America objecting to the use of barley for brewing beer instead of making bread. The war also prompted prejudice against Germans, who played an outsized role in the U.S. brewing industry.

Alaska voters passed the Bone Dry Act by a margin of two to one. That still left some residents unhappy about it. Harry's Grill, the site of the shooting, was one of many restaurants in Juneau that advertised "private boxes." They were booths with curtains that enclosed the table and seating, most likely to allow patrons to drink illegal booze with their meals.

For men like Prentice, prohibition meant a new and lucrative career in bootlegging. Prentice was an unattached young man who seemed unconcerned about morality or the law. Even before prohibition went into effect, his behavior had prompted another man to "take a shot at" him while at a local grocery store. A short newspaper article, which appeared in early 1917, said the shot "went wild and Prentice escaped injury."

In 1918, he was arrested for "having intoxicating liquor in his possession." He was fined $500 (the equivalent of $11,000 today) by the Commissioner's Court. His attorney, John R. Winn, appealed the ruling on his behalf. Prentice was later found "not guilty" in a jury trial. That same year, he was named "delinquent" for not reporting in as a draftee, one of only two men in Juneau who didn't report as ordered. He turned himself in and had a physical examination before being declared exempt from service.

He was arrested at least twice more, most notably for smuggling alcohol from Canada via the Taku River, south of Juneau. Bootleg liquor was found virtually everywhere during that time, manufactured in multiple stills in the area or smuggled from Canada, whose own prohibition was much more short-lived than Alaska's (it lasted just four years in British Columbia, ending in 1921).

In the fall of 1920, Prentice was a witness after officers arrested the Douglas federal marshal, George Johnson, for being associated with at least three boatloads of liquor from Canada. Prentice told a federal marshal that he and another man, Fred McGill, had crewed the boat, owned by Johnson, and that Prentice had helped fund, with Johnson, at least one of the shipments. The three shipments allegedly included forty-nine cases of liquor in June, 102 cases in August, and 132 in September. He also said that Marshal Johnson helped unload the boats in Douglas.

Prentice's candor resulted in his own indictment for possessing and selling illegal alcohol. Before he could come to trial, however, Johnson was tried.

It did not go well for the prosecutor. His main witness was Fred McGill, who had skippered the boat carrying the illegal cargo. He was not a good witness. A low point must have been when the U.S. District Attorney for Juneau (who was the prosecuting attorney's boss) was brought to the stand by the defense attorneys for Johnson. The District Attorney (John Smiser) took the stand to suggest that McGill was not trustworthy. The defense followed that with some well-respected Juneau and Douglas residents who testified that Deputy Marshal Johnson was "a law-abiding citizen" with a good reputation. Johnson himself testified that he had fired McGill for being a bad boat captain and had never had liquor aboard his boat except for two bottles for "private consumption." The jury acquitted Johnson.

Within a few months, the prosecutor dropped the case against Prentice as well. In the court filing, the prosecutor wrote, "the principal witness on behalf of the United States is one Fred McGill, who was entirely discredited as a witness on the trial of the above-named defendant George L. Johnson ... a successful prosecution cannot be maintained."

For Prentice, it was another escape from jail. Less than a year after the case was dropped, he and George Johnson, along with a third man, William Strong, started a company that supposedly planned to offer charter boat fishing and hunting on the Taku River. The Taku was one of the main avenues for bootleggers running alcohol from Canada, at the head of the river to Juneau was only about 20 miles from where the river enters the Pacific Ocean. The company was named the Taku Trading Company, a plain allusion to the thinly veiled bootlegging business bringing liquor down the Taku River to Juneau and Douglas.

That same year, 1922, Prentice was associated with a large still shut down by prohibition officers at Howard Point in Lynn Canal, west of Juneau. Officers reported the still was powered by a motor that allowed it to make fermented mash of up to forty-five gallons at a time. In addition to the still, the officers found five hundred gallons of mash being fermented, fifty sacks of brown sugar, and a "quantity of moonshine."

Although Prentice wasn't arrested in association with the still, he put up the $1,000 bail for the local man who was arrested, a fellow who went by the colorful name of Edward "Frozenfoot" Johnson.

Prentice branched out from Juneau in the illicit alcohol trade;

in early 1923, he was arrested in Cordova, a mining town northwest of Juneau. Again, the arrest included charges of assault against the officers who brought him in. An Alaska newspaper noted that Prentice "resisted so vigorously that the officers were compelled to use billies, fists and every available weapon to subdue him."

It became clear that Prentice had done more than sell alcohol and fight with police in Cordova when a local beauty salon owner in that town moved to Juneau in early 1922. Winnie Swanberg had been married to a prominent man in Cordova – the city clerk – before divorcing him in April 1922. At the time of the divorce, she was already living in Juneau with Prentice. The two referred to Winnie as Prentice's wife, although they weren't married, and she didn't take his name.

At some point, Prentice developed a friendship, or at least an acquaintance, with William Lott. It's possible it centered around bootlegging, based on the discovery police made in Lott's barber shop after his arrest for shooting Prentice. A piece of wall at the back of Lott's shop was found to be removable; behind it were 220 quarts of whisky, twelve quarts of vermouth, four of gin, three of cognac, and one of rum. Two other hidden spots were discovered, but both were empty. Lott denied both having purchased the alcohol from Prentice or even knowing it was there.

Lott and his wife, a Black woman and seamstress named Pauline, had lived in Juneau and the area for about nine years. The 1910 census shows them living in Umatilla, OR, and they were there through at least 1914. In Oregon, Lott worked as a railroad porter, and Pauline worked as a seamstress. There are no records either had children. Lott had been born in Paducah, Kentucky, around the time the Civil War ended. Kentucky had been an important border state but was mostly controlled by the Union during the war. It is possible his father was enslaved, since records indicate he was born in South Carolina.

After coming to Juneau, the Lotts spent more than a year in the mining town of Chichagof on Chichagof Island, about fifteen miles to the west. They returned to the Capital City in 1922 when Lott opened his own barber shop and public bath. Called the Arctic Bath House and Barber Shop, the business featured Turkish and steam baths as well as showers. It advertised "Large tubs and plenty of hot water at all times."

In 1920, Juneau had electricity throughout its downtown area, and an increasing number of businesses and residences were installing telephones, but indoor plumbing continued to be a luxury for many of the homes in the Territory's capital. Public baths were numerous and promised a variety of experiences, with businesses offering what they called "Roman," "Turkish," and "Russian" baths. Typically, the baths were open to both men and women, but they did not bathe together.

Lott had developed a reputation as a masseur and barber. He was also increasingly well known as what we would today call a sports therapist. The *Daily Alaska Empire* wrote a short article titled "Juneau Spirit is Shown by William Lott; Butler-Mauro." It noted that Lott, "popular barber and athletic trainer" had volunteered to work with baseball players in the City League. It went on to note:

"Mr. Lott has arranged for any of the ball players with sore arms, "charley horses," or ailments of that nature, to go to his establishment on Front Street and he will give them the proper treatment."

And then the shooting occurred. Although Prentice's killing was well covered by the local newspaper, there was surprisingly little speculation about why it occurred. It wasn't until the trial that Juneau residents had a glimpse into the relationship between the well-regarded barber and the disreputable bootlegger.

After Prentice succumbed to his wounds, Lott was quickly indicted by a Juneau grand jury for murder in the first degree. He hired William Faulkner as his defense attorney, the same lawyer used by the former Douglas federal marshal charged with bootlegging. Faulkner, a former deputy federal marshal himself, was probably the best-known defense attorney in Juneau. By 1923, he had practiced law for nine years. Lott was denied bail, so in July, he entered the federal jail, in the basement of the downtown courthouse, to await trial.

HARDING STARTS FOR ALASKA TODAY
"BILLY" PRENTICE SHOT BY BARBER

Headline in the *Alaska Daily Empire* the day following the murder, July 5, 1923

In November, he went before Judge T.M. Reed to plead not guilty. According to the newspaper, Lott "showed the same undisturbed calmness and lack of nervousness which had characterized his previous appearance in public since he was first arrested." It went on to say that he made his plea, "in a clear, distinct tone, audible in all parts of the courtroom."

The newspaper hinted that it may be difficult to find enough jury members who didn't know either Prentice or Lott, and the writer was correct. It took almost three days to seat a jury in early December 1923, and the court had to call three groups of potential jurors before it had enough to begin the trial.

Before it started, however, Faulkner asked Judge Reed to quash the grand jury indictment because the panel included three women and one Alaska Native, and Faulkner said they were not qualified to serve. Judge Reed quickly rejected the request at the time, but several months later, when the trial was over, he issued a lengthy opinion defending his decision in detail.

Judge Reed's defense is an illustrative glimpse into views of the time toward women and the indigenous population. He defended putting women on the jury by pointing to their right to vote. In Alaska, that had happened ten years before in 1913; the Nineteenth Amendment gave women nationwide the right to vote in 1919.

He concluded his defense of putting women on the jury by writing, "I cannot concede that in this day and age, especially after the adoption of the Nineteenth Amendment, that there is any rational basis for the exclusion of women from jury service on account of sex."

His defense of allowing an Alaska Native to serve on the grand jury reveals his prejudice toward indigenous people, likely reflecting attitudes of the time regarding the expectation that Alaska Natives must reject their culture in order to become full citizens of the U.S.

In the argument, Reed relied on a description of the particular juror, who he noted spoke and wrote English; had a business in Sitka, AK; and had "severed his tribal relations; had taken up his residence separate and apart from any tribe of Indians, and had adopted the habits of civilized life. He was, then, a citizen of the United States and the Territory, and qualified elector. It would have been error of the court, which would have been cause for quashing the indictment, to have dismissed this grand juror solely because he was not of the white race."

In December 1923, however, the focus wasn't on who the judge allowed on the grand jury, it was on the trial itself. In its first day of coverage, the *Alaska Daily Empire* noted that Lott "presented a calm, unworried appearance throughout the proceedings." His wife "has been at her husband's side in the court room."

The prosecution's case was led by Assistant U.S. District Attorney A. G. Shoup. It took two days to present, and Shoup brought ten eyewitnesses to testify about the shooting. They described "almost" no quarrel beforehand, except for Prentice calling Lott "a foul term." The reporter noted that the witnesses said the gunshots happened "quicker than those present could turn around in their seats."

The witnesses all testified they had not seen Prentice hit Lott prior to the shooting and had not heard much of the conversation between the two men, although four people testified that they heard Prentice call Lott "a lying son of a bitch." The witnesses included staff at the restaurant and those in the Prentice party, including his girlfriend, Winnie Swanberg, as well as other customers at the restaurant.

The patrol officer who arrested Lott, V.L. Tibbetts, said he was on his way to Harry's Grill after hearing the shooting and saw Lott on the street. The newspaper noted: "He testified he asked Lott what the trouble was and the former replied, 'I did it.' 'You did what?' asked Tibbetts. 'I shot Billy Prentice,' replied the negro."

Tibbetts said that Lott handed him the gun immediately and didn't seem very upset. Tibbetts took him to the jail in his automobile and asked Lott what happened. He said that Prentice called him, "a black son of a bitch," and he had to protect himself. (Lott later told the U.S. District Attorney that Prentice struck him in the face.) Officer Tibbetts said he smelled burning cloth during the drive, and when they arrived at the jail, Lott complained of stomach pain. It turned out that both his coat and trousers had been set afire by the gunshots. Lott had apparently fired the first shots into Prentice from his pocket. Witnesses said he pulled the gun from his pocket and fired the last bullet into Prentice as he lay on the floor.

Mrs. Ambler, who was washing dishes in the restaurant's kitchen, described seeing the shooting. She said she heard Prentice call Lott "a lying son of a bitch," and looked out, hearing the shots immediately afterward. She said that Prentice was facing the kitchen where she was working, with Lott's back toward her. After the initial shots, Prentice fell forward, against Lott. Then she saw an arm come up and Prentice fall to the ground. She ran into the back for several minutes, returning to see Prentice on the floor and Lott gone.

Roy Nolan, superintendent of the Juneau & Douglas Telephone Company, was seated at the restaurant's counter when the shooting occurred. The newspaper said his account was the most thorough. He said he had talked with Prentice shortly before Lott entered Harry's Grill, and Prentice was complaining about someone "double-crossing" him and needing to get a Dictaphone. A Dictaphone was an early recording device that allowed the user to dictate into a microphone, resulting in a record that could be used by a secretary to transcribe the dictation. It's a bit of a puzzle why Prentice thought he wanted one. Perhaps he thought it could record conversations, which it could not, unless both people spoke into the same microphone. It's difficult to imagine a bootlegger needing transcribed documents.

Nolan said he saw Lott enter at Prentice's invitation, and go to the back of the restaurant, where Prentice was hosting his group.

He said he noticed nothing unusual in either man's demeanor and turned to give his order. He said a minute or two later, he heard Prentice swear at Lott and, before he could turn in his chair, heard two shots. He said he turned to see Prentice with a hand on Lott's shoulder, having fallen against him. He said Lott backed up and Prentice fell to the ground. Lott then fired two more shots, the second shot after he pulled his gun from his pocket. That final shot was fired as Prentice lay on the ground.

Winnie Swanberg, Prentice's girlfriend, initially told the prosecutor she was married to Prentice but then admitted that they were only living as man and wife. She accused Lott of being "a gun packer" and said she and Prentice knew him well because they often frequented his bath house. She also said that Prentice used to own a gun, but it had been stolen recently.

Swanberg said Lott visited their apartment frequently and it was there that Lott had previously drawn a gun on Prentice. She said that Prentice took it from him, returning it before Lott left.

Four days prior to the shooting, Swanberg said Lott visited the apartment again and was "upholding the Negro race and finally asked her what she thought of negroes," according to the newspaper. She testified that she told him that she knew only that they were "lazy and dishonest." She said Lott then told her she had "been living with Billy Prentice too much" and pulled a gun that he laid on a table. She said her sister was present during this exchange. She also said that Prentice liked Lott and frequently said he "had a white heart." But, after hearing about his conversation with Swanberg, Prentice threatened to "knock Lott's head off when he saw him."

During cross-examination, she also admitted that she had been arrested for violating the Alaska Dry Bone Act in Cordova for drinking illicit alcohol.

On Friday, December 14, just two days after the trial began, the defense put on its case, relying heavily upon Lott, who took the stand in his own defense. The newspaper noted that the direct testimony – questioning by Lott's own attorney - took just forty minutes.

Before that, however, defense attorney Faulkner brought in twelve character witnesses. Seven testified as to the bad character of Prentice, describing him as "quarrelsome and violent." The exception to that testimony was patrol officer Tibbetts, who said, "since I've known him, he's been peaceful and quiet."

Five other witnesses, including a local doctor, testified to Lott as having "a good reputation as a peaceful citizen."

Once he was on the stand, Lott began by describing having met Prentice shortly after moving to Juneau nine years before. Prentice was a patron of his barbershop and bath house. The defendant said he was no more friendly with Prentice than he was with other patrons but had quarreled with Prentice in June, shortly before the shooting. He said he had met Prentice in his apartment and was given a drink of whiskey. Prentice then described a recent quarrel he had with Swanberg, during which he called his girlfriend "a vile name." Lott said he responded by pouring his drink on the floor, which angered Prentice. Lott said he feared Prentice, in part because he had seen him beat Swanberg to unconsciousness on one occasion. He also said he saw Prentice beat another woman in the past. (Winnie Swanberg later testified that Prentice had never done anything but "spank" her.)

Lott then described the eventful Fourth of July in detail. He said he had taken a bath at his shop and was walking to his apartment when he ran into Lloyd Winter, who knew Prentice. Winter (of the well-known photo studio Winter and Pond) warned Lott that Prentice was mad at Lott and "would knock my head off and wreck my joint," said Lott.

The barber then visited a shoe shining parlor before heading home. He was already carrying the pistol but had never fired it. He said he planned to walk to Salmon Creek (about four miles from downtown Juneau) and "try it out."

He went to a ball game, returning in a taxi with Winter and some other men. As he was leaving them downtown, he said Winter again called to him, warning him about Prentice. He returned home, had dinner and a nap, and got up in time to watch the parade at 7:00 p.m., followed by the fire hose races between fire departments before going to the City Cafe. At the City Cafe, he played a raffle game and won a small dice set. When he arrived home, his wife was in bed asleep. He woke her, and they played dice in bed. As he readied for bed, he said his wife asked him to go to the shop to get money to pay the rent. He did so and was returning home when Prentice called him into Harry's Grill.

The newspaper reported most of what happened next verbatim.

"Almost immediately, he said, Prentice put his hand on my shoulder and turned me around and said, 'Look at him, he looks like he is guilty!' He grabbed me and hit me. He put his right hand back of my neck like this (illustrating to the jury), and hit me here (on the jaw) with his left hand.

"'I asked him, guilty of what, Mr. Bill?' 'Of pouring that whiskey on the floor, you black son of a bitch,' he said, and with the words, he grabbed me and hit me.

"'I was scared,' continued the witness. 'I was scared he would get down on the floor and knock my eyes out and kill me. He was right on me.'"

Lott began shooting, his hand on the gun still in his pocket. Of his five shots, four hit the victim. He said the first shot was fired as the two men stood, breast to breast, with Prentice holding onto Lott's neck. Lott said he was afraid he had shot himself with the first shot because of the pain in his stomach caused by the burning cloth from the gunshot. He said Prentice kept pressing him backward until he was against the wall, and he felt so panicked that he doesn't recall the ensuing shots, including the final one at the prostrate Prentice. He also didn't recall shooting Prentice from his pocket, saying he didn't understand how his clothes got burnt.

Lott denied ever carrying a gun until the day of the shooting; he recalled the conversation with Swanberg about blacks but said he didn't have a gun at the time. He said he knew Prentice carried one on occasion because he had seen it when Prentice undressed for bathing at Lott's business.

On cross examination, he told District Attorney Shoup that he did own the liquor found in the false wall at his shop, the first time he admitted knowing of it. He denied getting it from Prentice, however, and said he had not done business with him.

Other defense witnesses included Lloyd Winter, the man who had warned Lott about Prentice. He said that earlier on July 4, he had seen Prentice downtown and Prentice had railed against Lott, "whom he cursed with great emphasis." Winter said he couldn't remember everything Prentice said against Lott but suggested he calm down. He also said he did warn Lott about Prentice but didn't remember saying that Prentice would beat Lott. The cab driver who dropped the men off after the ball game testified that he heard Winter warn Lott.

Other than Lott's testimony, perhaps the most surprising testimony was that of Federal Deputy Marshal Mort Truesdell, who recognized the gun that was taken off Lott when he was taken to the jail, where Truesdell was a guard. The marshal said it was his (the marshal's) gun.

He had loaned it to Lott to replace the barber's broken pistol. Truesdell said Lott kept a small gun in a drawer in his shop. Truesdell said he had put out the fire in Lott's clothes from the gunshot but did not confirm Lott's claim that Lott was spitting blood at the jail after being hit by Prentice.

(An interesting historical aside – the gun in question was originally owned by James Plunkett, the victim of notorious serial killer Edward Krause, who killed Plunkett in 1915.)

Another witness, Fred McGill (who sank the earlier prosecution against Prentice), also testified for the defense, saying he heard Prentice refer to Lott as "getting too smart."

The next day was the last day of the trial. Lott concluded his testimony, and both defense and prosecution attorneys presented closing arguments. Perhaps seeing the way the trial was headed, Assistant District Attorney Shoup stepped aside for another assistant D.A. to make the closing argument. Lester Gore told the jury that Lott was armed and prepared to shoot Billy Prentice. He said that Lott may have been worried about being beaten by Prentice, but that did not justify shooting him.

According to the newspaper, defense attorney Faulkner used his final comments to the jury to plead with its members "to allow no racial feelings to enter their deliberations." The reporter said his sympathetic portrayal of the hardships "of the Negro race" caused many women in the crowded courtroom to weep.

Before sending the jury to its deliberations, Judge Reed gave it the traditional instructions. These are typically tailored for each jury but often share common characteristics, depending on the case and the judge. Judges may also accept recommendations from prosecution and defense for the instructions. Defense attorney Faulkner's recommendations for the instructions and the judge's instructions are, somewhat surprisingly, included in the court records at the state archives in Juneau.

Judge Reed's instructions can be viewed as nothing but sympathetic to the defendant. He noted that the Lott "has offered direct evidence of his good reputation as a quiet and peaceful man." On the other hand, Prentice had the reputation "as a dangerous and quarrelsome man."

Reed told the jury that in proving the murder was not a murder due to self-defense, jury members did not need to determine whether Lott's life was really in danger, but only whether he had "reasonable cause to believe it to be in danger and so believed."

If Lott believed he was acting in self-defense, then the judge said he could not be convicted of murder. The jurors could consider the following options when coming to a verdict: first-degree murder with the death penalty, first-degree murder with life in prison, second-degree murder, manslaughter or not guilty.

After just three hours of deliberations, the jury came back with a verdict of not guilty.

Lott was promptly re-arrested for having illicit alcohol at his place of business. He was later convicted of bootlegging and

Titled *U.S. Marshals Clean Up*, this photo depicts federal marshals from Juneau at an illegal still they have found. *P344-260 Alaska State Library George Family Photo Collection*

sentenced to six months in jail and a $500 fine.

During his time in jail both before and after his trial for murder, Lott's Arctic Barber Shop and Bath House remained open under new management. Lott was able to resume operating the business after serving his sentence.

His death from a stroke in 1933 was in the newspaper with no mention of the Prentice case. Instead, it notes that the sixty-eight-year-old was "known to all the old-time pioneers of this district," and that he had operated a barber shop in several locations in downtown Juneau. It also commented on his support of ball players, saying he "was well thought of by the members of the teams."

Pauline Lott survived her husband but came to a dramatic and newsworthy end herself in 1936, when she was the final victim to die of a natural disaster in downtown Juneau.

Pauline, still working as a seamstress and living on Gastineau Avenue, was crushed by a piano in her house when it was hit by a

November mudslide that killed twelve people outright and three from the injuries they suffered. It is probably the deadliest natural disaster in the history of the Capital City.

Pauline passed away on Dec. 4, 1936, twelve days after the avalanche; she had spent those last days in the hospital. In its front-page coverage of her death, the newspaper noted she was married to William, who was well known. It adds: "Those who knew Mrs. Lott speak of her happy philosophy of life, which was expressed in doing kind deeds for others, and those for whom she worked speak of her honesty and integrity." There is no mention of her race. She and William are buried at Evergreen Cemetery in Juneau, as is William Prentice.

Chapter 6: Groceries and a Gunny Sack

Was it the canned peaches, the sardines, the gunny sack, or the note that convicted the killer of a Ketchikan fish buyer in 1930? The investigator, Thomas N. Henry, would probably say all of them. A special investigator with the U.S. Department of Justice, Henry was tasked with finding enough evidence to put away the killer of George P. Marshall, a fifty-eight-year-old fish buyer in Ketchikan.

Marshall was found dead aboard his anchored boat, the *Phoenix IV*, near Point Higgins, (about a dozen miles northwest of downtown Ketchikan) on Oct. 22, 1930. His hands and feet were tied up, and he was lying on the floor of the boat's galley. He had been shot through the foot and hit on the forehead. The autopsy showed he lived for an hour or so after being struck but died of a skull fracture. The boat's skiff and a strongbox containing cash were missing.

As a fish buyer, Marshall would travel to nearby fishing grounds to purchase from boats whose skippers were anxious to remain on the grounds, saving them trips into town to unload their catch. Because he paid the fishermen in cash, he often had large sums on board. But he usually did not anchor at Point Higgins because it wasn't close to where the boats were fishing. There were also witnesses who saw another man on the stern of the boat when it left Ketchikan.

Marshall was born and raised in Washington, D.C., but had come to Alaska about ten years before his death, most likely to work for the Kennicott Bonanza Copper Mine, his workplace in 1920. In 1924, he registered as the owner and master of a vessel in

Downtown Ketchikan. *P97-878 Alaska State Library Trevor Davis Photo Collection*

the territory of Alaska. In 1930, he was fifty-eight years old and had been operating the fish-buyer, the *Phoenix IV*, for several years.

Many people knew that Marshall had a metal strongbox attached with iron bolts to the floor of the *Phoenix*'s pilot house (from where the boat was operated). He had installed the safe after December 1929, when Harold Swegle of Ketchikan was indicted for stealing $721 from Marshall. The indictment again drew public attention to the five-foot-seven-inch older man who was often working alone while carrying large sums.

Just as in Petersburg, it was fishing that was the backbone of Ketchikan. Ketchikan's early human residents were the Taant'a (Tan-ta) Kwaan, which translates as Sea Lion Tribe. They're also known as the Tongass Tribe. They called the area where they settled Kitch.Kaaa, or Kichxaan. They were joined in the 1890s by the Sanyaa (sahn-ya) Kwáan, which means Secure In Retreat, Like A Fox In Its Den. Called the people of the Southeast wind, these Tlingits moved from Cape Fox, on the southern tip of the mainland near the British Columbia border, and settled in Saxman, just a few miles south of Ketchikan. Traditionally, Tlingits explored, hunted, fished, and lived in many parts of the area, as shown by the 136 Tlingit place names there.

In 1890, the census counted forty people in the town of Kichxaan. In 1900, the town, renamed Ketchikan by white settlers, had grown to 459 residents. It jumped to 3,520 in 1910, and by the time of our story in 1930, the population stood at 6,408, making it second only to Juneau's size in the territory.

In 1930, Ketchikan, along with the rest of Southeast Alaska, was in the midst of the second Alaskan "gold rush." This was when canneries were established throughout the sparsely populated islands and mainland of this portion of Alaska. In a sense, Ketchikan was at the center of this second economic boom – it was among the first places in Alaska to host a fish cannery and called itself the "Salmon Capital of the World." Canned salmon had become a staple of American pantries after the first cannery was opened in California in 1864. The popularity of canned salmon quickly outstripped the output of the salmon fishery of the west coast of the United States. Businessmen begin moving the industry north into Alaska, hiring Alaska Natives and Asian immigrants.

Ketchikan also depended on logging and milling, as well as the conveniences a larger community could offer to the surrounding villages and cannery towns. These included a radio station, newspaper, churches, a movie theater, and the brothels and small individual houses or "cribs" that made up the infamous Creek Street downtown. In 1930, prohibition still had three years before it ended, but Alaska residents had little trouble finding alcohol. They made their own or purchased bootleg liquor from Canada.

Today, Ketchikan remains the first stop for many people coming to Alaska, especially those aboard ships. While the first commercial flights began in 1927, steamships were still the way the majority of visitors came to the territory in 1930. The southernmost major port in Alaska, Ketchikan was not only the first stop for visitors, but also the only stop for many of those who came to the territory seeking work or adventure.

Alaska has always attracted people seeking adventure, as well as those escaping places, people or situations. Consequently, it has had more than its fair share of the transient men and women who saw Alaska as an opportunity to reinvent themselves. Many found themselves in Ketchikan without the money or desire to move further north. In 1936, the city police began the first fingerprint file in the territory, linking it with FBI records to identify those with criminal histories. The attempt was to slow down "the influx of bad men" into the territory, apparently with the assumption that their first stop would be Ketchikan before they went further north to commit crimes.

The March 24, 1936 edition of the *Nome Daily Nugget* stated:

"In the past Ketchikan has been something of a 'dumping ground' for the riff raff of the northwest states, being especially attractive to men wanting to get out of state. Steamer tickets for such men are most often made out only as far as Ketchikan because of low finances and the port has in the past had an unusually large number of undesirables, officers state."

The *Phoenix IV* some years after the murder, photographed in British Columbia.

Perhaps if police had checked the fingerprints of one of these men, Bert McDonald, his earlier convictions for burglary and escaping jail would have prompted more wariness. McDonald most likely arrived in Ketchikan in 1929, a fit, thirty-three-year-old man who was five-feet-ten-inches tall and weighed about 150 pounds.

It's unknown how McDonald connected with Lloyd Close in Ketchikan; perhaps Close had invited McDonald to Alaska or perhaps it was mere coincidence that the men, who had met while both serving time at the Walla Walla State Penitentiary in 1925, met again in Ketchikan five years later.

Close, who appears to have been living by his wits rather than a regular job, was residing with a woman he called his wife, although Ada Lundin was actually the wife of Bernard Lundin (as was revealed later when both Ada Lundin and Lloyd Close were charged with cohabitation in the state of adultery, a crime at the time).

In 1930, the former prison inmates, Close and McDonald, quickly joined forces and began commercial fishing together. McDonald was captaining the fishing boat, the *Comrade*, which belonged to a Captain Fowler, a resident of the coastal town of Stanwood, Washington, between Seattle and Bellingham. Fowler had befriended McDonald when Fowler visited the penitentiary at Walla Walla, WA. When McDonald was released, he stayed with Mr. and Mrs. Fowler and accompanied Captain Fowler on his boat, the *Comrade*, when Fowler went north to Alaska to fish. After they arrived in Ketchikan however, Fowler became ill and remained in the hospital for weeks, during which time McDonald fished with the *Comrade*. This was the boat that McDonald was living aboard when Close began fishing with him.

The first indication that anything had happened to George Marshall was a phone call and a note. On the evening of Tuesday, Oct. 21, 1930, a man came into Ferry's, a grocery, in Ketchikan and asked the owner, Ted Ferry, to call authorities and report that the *Phoenix* was in trouble at Point Higgins. Ferry was unable to reach anyone. That same evening, as the captain of the Coast Guard boat *Cygan* was waiting to go into the movie theater, he was given a note from his chief boatswain, who received it from a stranger who had walked aboard the docked *Cygan*. The note, written in pencil on lined paper said, "The *Phoenix IV* is in need of help – badly – laying in bite at Higgins Point. Go tonite! She is fish byer."

The next morning, the *Cygan* went to Point Higgins, found the *Phoenix* and the body on board, and towed the boat back to Ketchikan. (The newspaper said the Coast Guard had delayed leaving until the morning due to inclement weather. The captain also said he thought the note might be a hoax.) The *Cygan* was a submarine chaser, a class of Coast Guard boat built for use during WWI when German submarines were seen on the east and west coasts of the U.S. By the time the boats were built however, the war was over, so they were put into service to perform the more traditional services of the Coast Guard – law enforcement and maintenance of maritime signals and lights.

Once in Ketchikan, the body was autopsied, and the investigation began. It was found that Marshall's death was caused by a forehead contusion that fractured his skull. The town's coroner, accompanied by another man, searched the *Phoenix* for evidence of the bullet that apparently pierced the victim's foot. They found a bullet buried in the ship's deck, next to a hatch's edge. They chiseled it out, marked it with the coroner's initials and turned it over to the Department of Justice investigator.

Thomas N. Henry was stationed in the office of the Bureau of Investigation in Tacoma, WA. Five years after this murder, the Bureau of Investigation became the Federal Bureau of Investigation (FBI). Henry was sixty-five years old when he took on this case. Born in Missouri, he was a white-collar worker for much of his life. In 1910, he was a postmaster in Washington, D.C. It is likely he entered the bureau there, since he was a "salary worker" in Tacoma at the 1920 census and a special investigator in that city ten years later.

There were no immediate suspects, as evidenced by the unclaimed $500 reward offered by the city of Ketchikan, matched by a reward offered by the victim's estate. In November, the Alaskan newspaper in the nearby community of Petersburg, noted that the "Murder Mystery in Ketchikan Goes Begging." The newspaper said two unnamed suspects were being held in Juneau. It wasn't until February 1931 that another two suspects were arrested.

Somebody must have told investigators the name of someone who knew about the robbery and killing. In February, that person, who newspapers called a key witness, was located in Wyoming and escorted by a Wyoming sheriff back to Ketchikan. That witness, Kenneth Govro, implicated the two former convicts, Lloyd Close and Bert McDonald. Govro told of a conversation he overheard between the two men regarding the robbery, as well as being asked by McDonald to provide him with an alibi on the day of the murder. Govro also said he saw McDonald throw a heavy gunny sack into the ocean where the *Comrade* was tied up north of town.

Close was picked up in Ketchikan and quickly jailed, but it took a few weeks to find and arrest McDonald, who was found getting a medical checkup at a veteran's hospital in Portland, Oregon. He was promptly returned to Ketchikan, escorted by a federal special agent. It is an indication of the interest in this case that the newspaper reported 500 people were at the dock to get a glimpse of McDonald. They were mostly thwarted however; the agents kept him aboard for several hours before delivering him to a jail cell in the courthouse.

Close and McDonald were originally both charged with first-degree murder, but when the grand jury met in March, it indicted McDonald for murder. Although Close was also indicted, it was for an unrelated robbery. Neither Close nor Govro was indicted in the murder case, possibly because both agreed to testify against McDonald.

Date of Birth 2/29/96

d from McN**
From Leavenworth Age 38

1 1 5

Bert McDonald five years after being sentenced.

Physically, McDonald looked like an unlikely murderer – he had a thin, somewhat aesthetic face and needed glasses. He had a rough childhood but had no history of criminal activity as a youth. His parents, the Henmans, died when he was an infant, and he was put into the Seattle Children's Home. At age two, he was adopted by the McDonalds, a childless couple who also fostered a girl (although she wasn't adopted), who McDonald viewed as his sister. The family lived in Anacortes, WA. When he was nine years old, McDonald's foster mother died. His father was unable to afford childcare and worked long hours, so the two children were left alone a great deal.

McDonald left school after seventh grade, later saying he struggled in school but liked working with his hands. At fourteen, he took his first job at a local lumber mill and became a shingle weaver, making the cedar wood shingles that the Pacific Northwest popularized. He worked there sporadically, still living with his

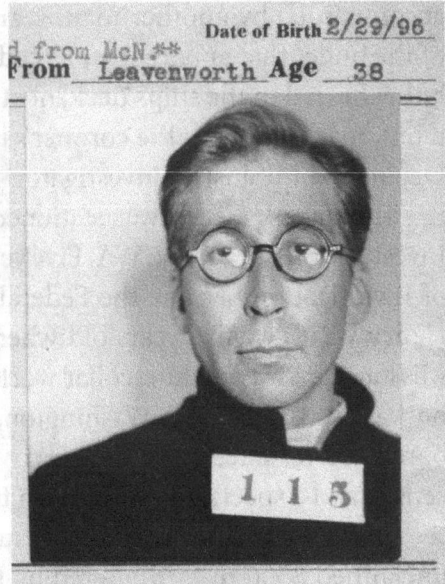

father, until he was twenty-one, when he entered the Army. It was 1917, and the United States had joined World War I. McDonald served overseas for eleven months and returned unwounded. He received an honorable discharge after serving a total of two years and returned to his father's home.

He spent some time running boats in Puget Sound but also worked occasionally as a shingle weaver. In 1920, he married eighteen-year-old Violet Bishop of Mount Vernon, WA, whom he had known for about six months. Although they remained married for two or three years, they separated two months after the marriage when the new husband was arrested on a charge of burglary. Violet quickly sought a divorce. McDonald spent fourteen months in the state penitentiary in Munro, WA. He was released in December 1921 and returned home to live with his father, with whom he had a contentious relationship. This is not surprising, given McDonald's propensity to keep returning home between jobs and prison sentences. In January 1923, a little more than a year after being released from prison, he was again arrested for burglary.

While awaiting legal proceedings in jail, he escaped. At his re-arrest, he was additionally charged with burglary and escape. He was sentenced to serve five to six years at the state penitentiary in Walla Walla, WA. In July 1929, he was released from the penitentiary and moved in with the Fowlers. From there, he accompanied Fowler on his boat, the *Comrade*, to Ketchikan to commercially fish.

The trial charging McDonald with first-degree murder began April 11, 1931, with jury selection. The prosecution was being handled by U.S. District Attorney Howard Stabler and assistant district attorney George Folta. Stabler was the DA for the First Judicial District, meaning he lived in Juneau and served as DA for all of Southeast Alaska. It was somewhat unusual for the District Attorney to take on a trial unless a victory was assured. This case must have been a safe bet for him. For the defense, the court named local attorneys George Grigsby and Harry McCain, since the defendant couldn't afford to hire lawyers.

The judge overseeing the case was Justin Harding. Harding is well known in Alaska for having made a key civil rights ruling in the territory in 1929. That case involved a part Tlingit girl, twelve-year-old Irene Jones, who began public school in Ketchikan in September 1929. Two days after starting, she was refused admittance to the school by Anthony Karnes, the school superintendent, who told her she must attend the Native school. Her parents, Paul and Nettie Jones, with the territory's first Alaska Native attorney, William Paul, Sr., appealed the decision, first to the school board and then to the courts.

In 1905, Congress established a territorial school system in Alaska to provide education for "white children and children of mixed blood who lead a civilized life." Based on this law, the Alaska Territorial Legislature established free schooling without a distinction in regard to race or color. The Ketchikan school board, however, had passed a resolution in 1928 that the school district would accept only those children "who are not acceptable to the United States Bureau of Education" (i.e., the Native school). This meant that Ketchikan schools would no longer accept any child of Alaska Native or Native American descent.

Judge Harding heard the case and ruled that the school board's resolution could not supersede the territory's law. Irene could return to the public school in Ketchikan. Her parents' legal fees should be paid by the school district.

Two years after that case, Judge Harding presided in McDonald's murder trial. The Ketchikan courtroom was in the courthouse located on the steep hillside above downtown. It is likely that McDonald was held in a cell in that building during the trial.

In his opening statement, the prosecutor said he would show that McDonald had hidden aboard the *Phoenix* before it left Ketchikan and then overpowered and tied up Marshall while searching for a key to the strong box. McDonald threatened violence against Marshall if he didn't give him the key, including shooting him in the foot. When Marshall didn't relent, McDonald used a hacksaw to cut the bolts holding the strong box to the deck, put it in the skiff on the *Phoenix*, and rowed away. Either before or after he cut away the strongbox, McDonald hit Marshall on the forehead, resulting in his death.

Prosecutor Stabler chose Charles Homan as his first witness. Charles was a friend of Marshalls and described driving Marshall around Ketchikan as the fish buyer prepared to leave for the fishing grounds on Oct. 20. Homan said he drove Marshall to the bank and said that Marshall withdrew about $1,100 in cash. He also took the fish buyer to the Tongass Trading Company to pick up a large quantity of groceries. The items purchased included small (half) cans of peaches, cans of Van Kamp pork and beans, and cans of sardines wrapped in green paper stamped with T. T. C. for Tongass Trading Company.

Other prosecution witnesses included two people who saw a second man on the stern of the *Phoenix* as it left Ketchikan; both testified that the man looked as if he could be McDonald. Dr. Mustard, the physician who performed the autopsy on the dead man, said he found black hair clutched in the victim's hand. McDonald had black hair. A forensic examiner for the Bureau of Investigation said the bullet found in the deck was the same caliber as the .38 revolver found on the *Comrade*.

The key witnesses for the prosecution were Lloyd Close and Kenneth Govro. Govro appeared to be another man living on the edge in Ketchikan. He was friendly with both Marshall and McDonald; he had met the latter when needing a boat tow. At the time of the murder, Govro had been living aboard the *Comrade* with McDonald for several days. On the 20th, the day of the murder, Govro had walked into town with a rifle he intended to sell. After pawning it for $5, he got a meal and played pool, returning late to where the *Comrade* was tied to a dock near the sawmill north of town. He testified that McDonald arrived at the boat shortly afterward with Close. He said that McDonald threw a small burlap sack onto the bunk. Inside it were small cans of peaches, Van Kamp pork and beans, and sardines with the T. T. C. stamp. He also testified that he had seen McDonald with a .38 revolver he believed belonged to Close.

Close testified that McDonald had once mentioned to him that the *Phoenix IV* was a place they could get "easy money" and on another occasion, said he thought Ketchikan would be a good place for a "peat man" (someone who breaks into safes). On Oct. 5, he said McDonald told him "let's stick up the old bird on the *Phoenix*." On the night of the murder, Close found McDonald walking on the road near the sawmill north of Ketchikan, using a flashlight to see the way. He gave McDonald a ride to the *Comrade*, which was tied up near the sawmill. He said McDonald was carrying a bag of groceries, and described seeing the same items mentioned by Govro. He also said that McDonald told him, "If anyone asks you, tell them I was on the *Comrade* all day."

Another prosecution witness was the grocer who sold McDonald food and with whom he had a line of credit. He testified that his store didn't carry the small (half) cans of peaches, the Van Kamp brand of beans, or the T. T. C. stamped sardines. The Tongass Trading Company owner testified that he carried the half can of peaches specifically for Marshall; he didn't recognize McDonald as a customer.

Govro also testified that he saw McDonald throw a heavy gunny (burlap) bag into the ocean near the *Comrade*'s spot on the dock near the sawmill. The chief federal investigator, Henry, was brought to the stand to testify that he sent a diver to the spot where Govro said McDonald had thrown the bag into the ocean. The diver had found parts of an acetylene torch in the water, as well as 42 hacksaw blades and the rotting gunny bag.

Govro said the defendant had asked him to support his alibi for the day of the murder. McDonald told him that his alibi was that he, McDonald, had visited friends to collect some sheet music he had loaned them (they weren't home) and then returned to the boat, where he had spent the rest of the day with Govro. Govro said in actuality, he hadn't seen McDonald until late in the evening.

In cross-examination, defense attorney Grigsby asked Govro if he had given a note to the *Cygan* crew member or called the authorities from Ferry's store. He said he had not.

Upon rebuttal from the prosecutor, Govro said that after he and McDonald heard about the hair in the dead man's hand being found in the autopsy, McDonald no longer went into town during daylight hours.

At this point, Stabler rested the prosecution's case. Defense Attorney Grigsby then asked the judge for acquittal from the jury, stating that the evidence had not shown a connection between the theft and the murder and that the evidence was insufficient to prove the case. The judge dismissed his request.

The two defense attorneys had little to work with, so they tried to plant doubt in the jury about the prosecution's case. Grigsby brought in two witnesses who claimed they had seen objects thrown from the *Phoenix* at different points on the 20th, apparently trying to show that Marshall himself may have thrown items overboard. There was also an odd exchange regarding the black hair that had been found in Marshall's clenched hand. Although investigator Henry said the hair had been examined by a forensic expert associated with his office and that hair had been collected from McDonald, the prosecutor objected to further questions on the topic. The judge upheld the objection.

The prosecutor also objected to questioning Ted Ferry, the grocery store owner, about identifying the man he saw in the store the night of the 21st. Again, the judge upheld the objection. It's unclear why both these objections were upheld, especially since they could have built a stronger case for the prosecution if the man in the store and the hair had been connected to McDonald. One can only assume that the answer to both questions would have led away from McDonald, thus helping the defense. The question is why the objections were upheld – perhaps the two identifications were so unclear as to simply complicate matters.

Defense attorneys brought in Lloyd Close to counter the evidence by Govro; specifically, he was asked whether Govro had been around the house of Close's brother, where the Colt revolver was kept, or around the shed behind the house, where an acetylene torch was stored. Govro denied ever being in the area; Close said he had seen him near the shed. Close also said the revolver never left the house, testimony supported by his brother and sister-in-law.

Finally, the defense put McDonald on the stand. He denied any involvement with the murder, the gun or the gunny sack found in the ocean. He said he spent the two evenings when the *Phoenix* was at anchor at Point Higgins waiting out the road for Close, who was supposed to meet him there so they could look for a cache of liquor that was supposed to be there. He said he and Close found it and sold it to a taxi driver, which is how he got the money to leave town. He refused to identify the cab driver during earlier questioning and on the stand, saying he didn't want to "implicate anyone." This was during prohibition, so it was illegal to buy or sell alcohol.

The defense then rested, but not without Grigsby again saying there was not enough evidence to proceed with the charges and calling Stabler and assistant District Attorney Folta, "the most unscrupulous attorneys in the Territory of Alaska."

It was now time for Judge Harding to instruct the jury. The instructions were very even-handed, focusing on the need to look at the evidence and weigh the testimony. He noted that federal law required that a death caused during a robbery be only considered first-degree murder. He wrote:

"I have heretofore instructed you that in order to find the defendant guilty of murder in the first degree you must find the robbery charged in the indictment was committed, and therefore that you must find each and every essential element of such robbery beyond a reasonable doubt."

Therefore, murder committed during a robbery could not be considered either second-degree murder or manslaughter. The jury could only choose among not guilty, guilty of first-degree murder with capital punishment, or guilty of first-degree murder with a life sentence.

On April 24, the jury came back with a verdict of guilty of

first-degree murder without capital punishment. Judge Harding imposed a life sentence "at hard labor" in a hearing on May 2, 1931.

McDonald was first sent to McNeil Federal Penitentiary on an island outside of Seattle. Two months later, he was transferred to Leavenworth Penitentiary in Kansas, which was routine at the time for Alaska prisoners, all of whom began their sentences at McNeil. In Leavenworth, his record shows multiple infractions, several of them around him refusing to work or obey orders. He also "fought in the library" and "showed disrespect to officer and ... insolence in band room."

The Leavenworth record notes that McDonald was of a quiet nature and rarely socialized with others. "He seems to enjoy playing his saxophone during band hours, which seems to complete any desire for recreation or other type of entertainment." His previous jail escape, however, continued to haunt him, and possibly led to his transfer to Alcatraz in 1934. Alcatraz Federal Penitentiary, on an island in San Francisco Bay, was considered to be a place where escape was impossible.

In Alcatraz, his behavior was generally good, according to records. Within a few weeks of arriving, he asked for permission to put a shelf in his cell and to fix up the band room. Later, he successfully asked for a saxophone and magazine subscriptions to *Sunset, Popular Mechanics,* and *Outdoor Life.* He also asked for a notebook for a correspondence class he was attending. All the requests were granted.

In 1939, he wrote a lengthy letter to prison officials, denying his involvement in a recent food strike and asking for his work privileges to be reinstated. At the time, he was working in the prison's furniture shop, where he wrote that he had overseen the construction of more than one hundred pieces of furniture. He ended the letter by saying he would do other work if necessary. He said he wanted to keep a clean record for the next six years, when he would be eligible for parole.

"I'm not particular as to where I work, all I want is to continue with my music," he wrote.

In 1944, McDonald's behavior had been good enough that he was transferred back to McNeil Island after ten years at Alcatraz. In 1946, he had his first opportunity at parole but failed to receive it. One of the board members noted the FBI report of the crime:

"showed that subject began to deliberate and plan the robbery which resulted in the murder herein more than 2 months before he committed it, and that, although a twice-made proposal on his part to a fellow fisherman, one Lloyd Close, to assist him in committing the crime met with refusal and with words of pity, describing the intended victim, George P. Marshall, 'as an old and deaf man who has had enough bad luck already,' but he had clung to his felonious purpose and in committing the robbery upon an aged man, alone on his boat, upon which subject had hidden away for hours, perpetrated a very brutal murder."

The board member concluded: "Even though this man is serving a life sentence we believe he must be classified as a very poor risk and we recommend his application be denied."

Before the parole board in 1959, possibly in order to sway the board, McDonald said, for the first time according to prison records, that he had killed Marshall. He said that:

"while he boarded this man's boat for the purpose of committing robbery, he had no intention whatsoever of using violent tactics, which he engaged in by virtue of this man's attempt to resist his activities in the commission of the robbery, which was his primary motive. He admits he hit this man over the head with a blunt instrument in the course of the scuffle when the two engaged in while he was attempting the robbery, and that he thereafter left him on the deck, threw the safe off the boat and placed it in the dingy, which he had used for the purpose of getting aboard the boat, thereafter opening the safe on the shore, and extracting, therefore, approximately $1,000."

This accounting does not match the testimony at the trial, which placed him on Marshall's boat while it was in Ketchikan. It's also interesting that he didn't say what he hit Marshall with and insinuated he hit Marshall in the back of the head, which was

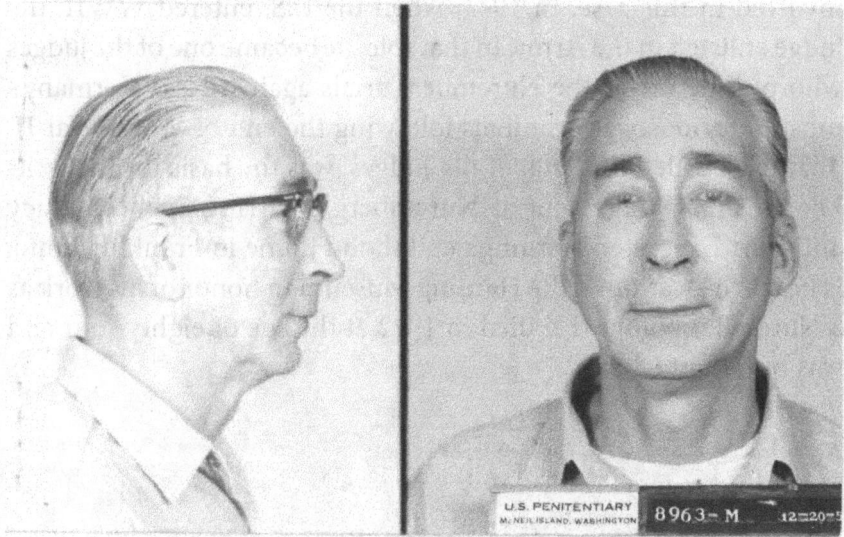

Bert McDonald in 1950, eleven years before being paroled.

inaccurate. He also left the man in the galley, not the deck, and described "a scuffle," rather than tying the man up and shooting him through the foot. And finally, he didn't admit to taking the skiff off the *Comrade*.

The most likely explanation for the conflict between his accounting and the truth is that he wanted to downplay his actions during the robbery and murder. It's hard to tell from this vantage point, but given that the strongest testimony against him was from two men just as hard up as he was, it raises some doubt of his acting alone.

In 1961, McDonald was paroled to the Western Region of Washington. Prison officials found him a job in a furniture store, and a Catholic chaplain found him a place to live. He asked to be placed where he could build boats, but the prison officials were reluctant to have him work where he could so easily leave the area. McDonald, now sixty-five, began working at the S.F. Harmon Manufacturing Company when he was released in 1961. He only had seven years of freedom before dying in 1968 at age seventy-two. He was buried in Tacoma.

Judge Harding had perhaps the most celebrated life of anyone

involved in this case. In 1941, when the U.S. entered WWII, the
judge enlisted in the Army. In that role, he became one of the judges
who presided over the Nuremberg trials against Nazi Germany's
most notorious war criminals following the end of World War II.
That trial, called the Trial of the Judges, was the basis for the well-
known film "Judgement at Nuremberg," starring Spencer Tracy
and Burt Lancaster. Harding's childhood home in Franklin, Ohio,
is now the location of the Harding Museum in honor of his work as
a Nuremberg judge. He died in 1972 at the age of eighty-four and
was buried in Ohio.

Chapter 7: The End of a Boy Hero

LeRoy Vestal was fifteen years old when he became the youngest Alaska soldier on the front lines of World War I. He served in the Fifth Field Artillery and then the 109th Tank Battalion, where he was wounded. He was also among the first injured soldiers to return to the United States after the armistice of 1918. At seventeen years old, the wounded veteran came back to his hometown of Juneau and started his second year of high school.

Fifteen years later, the then thirty-one-year-old was killed with one bullet by a bakery clerk in her boarding room in downtown Juneau. It was an ignominious end to a celebrated war hero, father, and well-known Juneau resident.

Vestal was the only child born to Frank and Ann Vestal. Ann Doneghy was just seventeen years old when she married the twenty-eight-year-old barber Frank Vestal in Juneau, Alaska, in 1901. Frank Vestal was known well enough in Juneau to be featured in an article in the *Douglas Island News* in 1900, noting that he was an officer in the newly formed Independent Order of Bachelors. (The article includes the unappetizing dinner enjoyed by the bachelors consisting of halibut stew, seaweed cake, boiled salmon bellies, hard tack, and onions.)

LeRoy was born two years after his parents wed. The young couple continued to be included in social notes. In April 1905, the *Douglas Island News* wrote that "a crowd of young folks [40 people were named] raided the home of Mr. Frank Vestal, the occasion being the 19th birthday anniversary of his brother-in-law, Mr. Thomas S. Donaghey. The girls brought good things to eat, and the boys brought Tom a nugget watch chain as a token of esteem."

By 1910 however, the marriage was over. The census states that Frank Vestal was living with his parents in Newberg, Oregon, and his son, then seven-year-old LeRoy, was part of the Oregon household. Ann was working as a housekeeper in Fairbanks, AK.

Newspaper accounts indicate LeRoy Vestal often spent the school year with his mother and the summers with his father. Based on steamship passenger lists, it appears he was making the lengthy trip from Oregon to Alaska alone at the age of eleven. His mother remained in Fairbanks until 1912, and LeRoy stayed with her there for at least one school year.

After returning to Juneau in 1914, Ann met and married Ray George Day, who worked in the print department of the town's

LeRoy Vestal in his freshman year at the University of Washington.

daily newspaper, *The Daily Alaska Empire*. As described in the newspaper, the December 1914 wedding was an unexpected event.

The newspaper noted:

"The marriage was a real surprise to Mr. Day's fellow workers on *The Daily Alaska Empire* and to a large circle of friends of the couple in town. Mr. Day last Monday asked for a vacation of a week without 'batting an eyelash.' He confided to no one the real secret of his heart, and only the visit of Rev. Stevens to the St. George House neighborhood last evening led to the discovery that Mr. Day had 'put one over' on his friends."

Mrs. Day continued to be a noted figure in social events described in the newspaper. She also worked outside the home, at one time managing the Bergman Hotel in downtown Juneau. Her husband stayed at the newspaper, perhaps one reason the family's activities were frequently mentioned there. Roy Day also served as a member of the Juneau City Council for some time.

LeRoy had completed his first year of high school when he enlisted. It's unknown what prompted the decision. Since he had been traveling independently between Oregon and Alaska for several years, he may have felt confident that he could handle himself as an adult. In May 1917, three days after his fifteenth birthday and just a month after the United States entered WWI, he stopped in Seattle en route to Oregon and enlisted in the U.S. Army.

According to an article in the Juneau paper, LeRoy's mother learned of his enlistment after receiving a postcard from her son, stating he was at Fort Bliss, Texas and expected to leave for France within a few weeks. His confidence led him to add to the postcard that after going to France, "we are going to Berlin."

What is most puzzling about this article and ensuing stories of LeRoy's exploits as a soldier is that neither of his parents made any attempt to tell the Army his real age. At the time, only men eighteen or older could legally enlist. If either of his parents had contacted the Army with his birth certificate, he would almost certainly have been sent home, as other underage enlistees were. Neither parent took any action.

We know something of LeRoy's service during WWI due to an article that appeared in a San Francisco newspaper in December 1918. The author, Elenore Meherin, interviewed LeRoy while he recuperated in the Letterman Army Hospital in California. She wrote:

"Corporal LeRoy Vestal, perhaps the youngest boy to have fought in the American ranks, was but 15 when he left Juneau, Alaska, for service in France. He was 16 when he volunteered for the tank service, and early in September was placed in charge of a 'Baby Tank' in the St. Mihiel sector at the start of the big American drive."

A "Baby Tank" was a two-person tank that had been created by the French and was to play a key role in the Allied battles against the Germans during the war. LeRoy describes his tank being one of two advancing through the German lines in the Argonne Forest in September 1918. Behind them, Allied soldiers advanced. LeRoy told the reporter:

"We had ploughed our way through one town and were just approaching the second when I heard a terrific explosion. I knew that it had hit the other tank and that the German fire would be concentrated on us.

"We were already within the German lines. Our own men were 500 yards behind us. Then came a clang that might have split the earth in two. It was a German 77 [field gun that shot three-inch shells] and it struck with a shocking force against our engine. We only carry nine liters of gas so you can imagine what a pretty flare-up we made.

"In five seconds, our tank was a mass of flames. A piece of the shell tore through the stomach of the driver. He collapsed as though he had been broken in two. But he wasn't dead. I talked to him and pulled and dragged him free from the wrenched and twisted steel.

"It was a horrible thing to do. Every pull I gave sent agony clean through him. The flames were reaching out and licking our faces. The German shells were dropping everywhere. We were almost at a big hole gouged in the earth."

LeRoy then described the painful death of the tank driver, and his own attempt to get back to the other soldiers.

"Machine gun bullets were peppering all about us – the pal that was dead and me lying wondering which way to crawl back to our men. I'd just started out when three of the bullets hit me. I hopped and crawled and ran and I got to the first aid station somehow."

LeRoy's war record was recognized when he received the Purple Heart. While awarded now only to soldiers wounded in war, the Purple Heart during WWI was also awarded for meritorious conduct.

The teenager received a hero's welcome in his hometown when he returned in February 1919 after spending several months in the California veterans' hospital. The *Daily Alaska Empire* reported: "Greeted with the cheers of his friends and former schoolmates, LeRoy Vestal, son of Mr. and Mrs. R.G. Day, returned to his home on the *Princess Mary* [steamship] this morning after giving nearly two years – mostly in France – in the service of his country."

A month after returning to Juneau, LeRoy Vestal was a guest of honor at a dinner hosted by six high school girls, including the sisters Nadja and Sasha Kashevaroff. There were five other teen boys also invited. "The table was prettily decorated and shaded candles shed a rosy glow over the whole," the paper noted.

The transition back to being a high school student appears to have been difficult. Although LeRoy should have started back as a sophomore, he appears to have spent the remaining school year as either a sophomore, junior, or senior; he is called each at some point in the newspaper. He was a football star and played basketball for the high school team. He had some medical issues. Six months after returning home, he went to Anchorage for an unidentified surgery. The

Nadja Kashaveroff's high school senior photo as it appeared in the *Alaska Daily Empire*.

following fall, he had his appendix removed in an emergency surgery in Juneau.

There were only ten graduates from Juneau High School in 1920, and Vestal is not among them. He appears to have stopped attending school in 1920 but continued with an active social life. He refereed for basketball games and was a frequent guest at social events. He also took a summer job with a surveying crew working in northern Alaska and was twice elected Messenger for the Alaska Territorial Legislature, serving a role we would now call a legislative page.

Many of the social events he attended included a 1920 graduate, Nadja Kashevaroff. Nadja was the daughter of Father Andrew Kashevaroff, a local Russian Orthodox priest and historian. She was one of six daughters of the priest and his wife, Martha. Martha Bolshania was Alaska Native, a Tlingit from the Kiks.adi Clan in Sitka. Father Kashevaroff was also part Alaska Native – Unangan – and Russian.

The Kashevaroffs were well known in Juneau; their daughters often appeared in social notes describing their theatrical and musical performances. Nadja was also a noted basketball player for the high school. The year she was elected editor-in-chief of the school newspaper, LeRoy was elected athletic editor.

At least two of Nadja's sisters garnered national attention in some circles because of their unconventional approaches to life. The two women, Xenia and Sasha, were associated with a bohemian group in Carmel, California. The group included Ed Ricketts, the marine biologist whose character is featured in John Steinbeck's book, *Cannery Row*, as well as Steinbeck himself, and Joseph Campbell, who later earned acclaim as an author and mythologist. Sasha was married to Jack Calvin, a friend of Rickett's; Calvin was an author and sailor. Xenia married the avant-garde composer John Cage and was herself an artist. The group was known for sexual adventures and became somewhat notorious.

After graduating from Juneau High School in 1920, Nadja Kashevaroff took a job teaching in Wacker (Ward Cove), near Ketchikan. After teaching there for one school year, she returned to Juneau for the summer vacation. Her sister, Sasha, spent the school year teaching in the Haida village of Kasaan on Prince of Wales Island, and the two young women reunited for the summer. In late July 1921, the sisters left for Berkeley, California, where Sasha entered her second year in college; Nadja was to be a freshman.

LeRoy continued to be featured in social notes; in December 1920, he was a referee at a Juneau vs. Douglas basketball game. In March 1921, he was appointed

JUNEAU BOY IS GETTING SPACE IN NEWSPAPERS

Life-Size Photo of LeRoy Vestal Appears in the Leading San Francisco Papers.

SPECIALLY INTERVIEWED

He Was in the Thick of the Fighting in Argonne Forest and Gives Some of the Details.

Headline in the *Alaska Daily Empire* Dec. 30, 1918.

librarian for the court system. In August 1921, he attended a farewell party for a friend. The next month, he himself moved to Seattle to attend the University of Washington. The following February, LeRoy was named assistant business manager for the university's newspaper. In June 1922, he was named vice president of the upcoming sophomore class. The same note said that LeRoy would be spending the summer with his mother and stepfather in Juneau before returning to school in the fall.

The first mention of what happened next was in a March 1923 edition of the *Alaska Daily Empire of Juneau*. LeRoy's mother and stepfather said they had received notice of a seven-pound baby boy being born to Mr. and Mrs. LeRoy Vestal. Three months later, a social note stated that Mrs. Day was leaving Juneau to attend an Eastern Star conference in Tacoma and to visit her son and daughter-in-law in Seattle. A month after his mother sailed for Seattle, LeRoy left Juneau for the same destination. It is unclear how long he had been in town.

So, sometime after Nadja left for school in Berkeley, CA in July 1921, she and LeRoy saw each other, she got pregnant, and the by-now-married couple had a son. Leroy Vestal Jr., was born twenty months after Nadja left to attend college; she would have become pregnant in June 1922.

According to later accounts, Nadja and LeRoy became a couple when they were both at the University of Washington. This seems unlikely, however, since she left to attend college in California, and the newspaper does not mention her changing schools. When they married is unclear; there are no marriage records to be found and no mention in Alaska or Washington newspapers about the union.

In early June 1922, the Juneau newspaper wrote that Mrs. Day would be gone for several weeks, but she returned after just two weeks with her daughter-in-law, Nadja, and her three-month-old grandson. Within a week, LeRoy left Juneau for Seattle, most likely to pack and ship household goods, or perhaps just to get out of town when his wife and son arrived.

In late July, the *Daily Alaska Empire* wrote that Nadja and her son had been in Juneau for several weeks visiting family. LeRoy Vestal, who had evidently remained in Seattle, was now due to arrive in Juneau within a week.

Despite the attention given to LeRoy and Nadja in the past, the newspaper had apparently not received notice of a wedding, since the note about Mrs. Day visiting her daughter-in-law and son was the first public announcement of the couple's marriage. After Vestal's death, his obituary stated that he and Nadja had begun seeing each other because they were both attending college in Seattle. The marriage and birth marked the end of college for Nadja and LeRoy.

The young couple and their son remained in Juneau, initially living with LeRoy's mother and stepfather. They continued to be part of Juneau's social scene; Leroy Jr. was a noted guest at a "baby birthday party" in August of 1923.

In 1925, LeRoy's mother and stepfather moved to Florida, where they purchased a printing press. The older couple had prospered in

Juneau; they owned real estate and had "business interests," the newspaper reported. There was also a passing mention of health issues experienced by Mrs. Day, which may have prompted the move.

The Days, however, continued to visit Juneau regularly. It appears that, like many snowbirds today, the Days spent winters in Florida and summers in Juneau with

LeRoy Vestal, Jr.'s high school senior photo.

the Vestals. In 1930, Nadja and LeRoy purchased a summer home in Fritz Cove, about a fifteen-mile drive from downtown Juneau. The commute was lengthy enough (and probably had unplowed roads during the winter) that Juneau families typically used homes "out the road" as summer places, returning to town in the fall and winter.

The *Daily Alaska Empire* in mid-May 1933 wrote about these summer homes in an article titled "Annual Exodus to Country is Well Underway: Juneau People Forsake Town for Country Roads on Highway." LeRoy Vestal is listed among those who relocated for the summer.

In January 1931, the Days were in Florida but expected to reside with the Vestals in the summer. That summer visit to the Vestals would have been complicated by fifty-six-year-old Frank Vestal's decision to move from Oregon to also live with his son and daughter-in-law in Juneau. Although the newspaper suggested this was a permanent move, Frank was living in Oregon again two years later. It's likely that the young couple, Frank, his ex-wife and her husband might not have made for a comfortable household.

In May of that same year, the household received another parental visit. Nadja's father, A.P. Kashevaroff, spent about ten days recovering from an illness at the home of his daughter and son-in-law.

In fall 1932, the newspaper noted that both the Days and Vestals moved from what must have been their winter apartment residence to the Wickersham House on 7th Street in downtown Juneau. In that same month, Nadja and her son accompanied her mother-in-law and father-in-law on a trip south. During the young couple's marriage, the newspaper frequently made reference to Nadja Vestal and her mother-in-law traveling together. Usually accompanied by Leroy Jr., the two women sailed south and occasionally north. There was no mention of LeRoy and Nadja traveling together.

Both Nadja and LeRoy, however, remained active in Juneau life. At twenty-nine, Nadja was elected Assistant Secretary of the Alaska Territorial House of Representatives. After his marriage, LeRoy worked at the *Daily Alaska Empire* and later at the Alaska Juneau Gold Mining Company. In 1927, he was hired as Chief Clerk with the Steamboat Inspection Service. This job entailed frequent and lengthy travel, as he was often part of a team that went around the territory inspecting steamships.

LeRoy also spent much of his free time with the American Legion. He was one of the veterans who began Juneau's chapter of the national organization after returning home. Much of the newspaper society notes that refer to LeRoy in later years were activities related to the Legion.

The American Legion was started nationwide in 1919 with a group of American veterans who convened in Paris. Later that same year, the organization was named the American Legion and was chartered by the U.S. Congress. The speed of its creation and popularity throughout the country was almost certainly the result of thousands of young war-weary veterans returning to their homes in a country that seemed little impacted by a war that had torn apart Europe.

The American Legion became instrumental in efforts to improve medical care for veterans, resulting in the U.S. Congress creating the precursor to the Veterans Administration. It also supported and helped create chapters of the Boy Scouts of America and worked on efforts to prevent desecration of the American flag (American Legion chapters continue to accept old flags for proper disposal).

LeRoy was a strong advocate for veterans and held several information sessions for veterans on government benefits. Among other activities, the American Legion, when led by LeRoy, sent letters to all ex-service men in the Juneau area about those benefits, including veterans of World War I and the Spanish-American War. He also spearheaded an effort to place headstones on the graves of each veteran in Juneau.

In addition to his advocacy for veterans, LeRoy was involved in local dramatics and theatrical presentations. In 1927, the American Legion put on *Oh, You Wildcat*, which the newspaper called "the funniest comedy ever produced in Juneau." LeRoy was "master of technicalities" behind the scenes and played a minor role on the stage. Another American Legion production in 1929 listed him in charge of press and publicity for the comedy *Cappy Ricks*.

Nadja Vestal was also involved in some performances as a singer, but there is no mention of the couple ever performing at the same event. LeRoy often spent much of the summer months traveling for work inspecting steamships and traveled frequently on American Legion business. Nadja and their son also left town, often for weeks or even months, to visit either her in-laws or her sisters. Based on steamship passenger lists, the couple may have spent much of each year apart, especially between 1930 and 1933.

In June 1933, just a month after the newspaper wrote that he had moved to the Fritz Cove home for the summer, LeRoy moved from his house and was living in a local hotel. The following month, his mother hosted an event for the Martha Society of the Presbyterian Church at the Vestal home. The newspaper noted that Mrs. Day was now making her summer residence at the Vestal home.

At some point, between LeRoy leaving home and his death, he and Nadja divorced, and he began seeing a young divorced woman named Astrid Pedersen Crowell.

Astrid Pedersen was a slender woman with brown hair who immigrated from Norway to the United States in 1923 at the age of twenty. In leaving Norway, she left behind a three-year-old son, Bjorne Pedersen. It appears the son was illegitimate, since there is no record of a marriage, and the child went by Astrid's maiden name and lived with her parents.

Between arriving in New York in December 1923 and November 1924, Astrid traveled to Alaska and got married to a nineteen-year-old man from South Dakota named Stephen Sallee Crowell. They wed in Ketchikan on Nov. 5, 1924. How they met or how long the couple was in Ketchikan is unknown.

By July 1929, the couple had moved to Juneau. Stephen operated a shoe repair shop downtown, and twenty-six-year-old Astrid worked as a waitress in local restaurants before being hired as a clerk at the Peerless Bakery, also downtown. The couple had no children.

Astrid was "highly regarded" by her employers at the bakery, according to a later newspaper account. She was described as "quiet, well-mannered and unassuming" with "a pleasant and agreeable disposition."

It's easy to imagine that LeRoy, working downtown at his steamship job, noticed the pretty clerk at the bakery and struck up a conversation. It's just as easy to speculate that Astrid was impressed by the thirty-year-old war hero. In February 1933, Astrid and Stephen Crowell divorced.

From today's perspective, a divorce in 1933 may seem unlikely or unusual. But in Juneau, divorces were not uncommon; each quarter, the newspaper noted a number of divorces that had been granted during the preceding three months. This divorce, however, received no notice in either court records reported in the newspaper or among its social notes.

Astrid and LeRoy "had been friendly for several months," according to the newspaper on Dec. 29, 1933. Two days before, on Dec. 27 a Wednesday, Astrid called in sick to her job and then went to her bank, where she closed her account and took out more than

$400 in savings. The next day, she called LeRoy Vestal and asked him to come to her room in the boarding house of Dr. G.L. Barton on Gastineau Avenue. Dr. Barton had at least one other tenant in the building – a family residing in a four-room apartment.

Vestal left his office at 4:00 p.m. and arrived at the Barton residence about 4:30 p.m. Dr. Barton admitted him, and Vestal went to Astrid's room. About ten minutes later, the other tenants in the home heard gunshots. At the same time, Astrid's former brother-in-law, Wesley Crowell, was greeted at the door of the home by Dr. Barton. Crowell was hand-delivering a Christmas card for Astrid. Dr. Barton took the card to Astrid's room and knocked on the door. Getting no response, he opened it.

His first sight was the body of LeRoy Vestal, lying on the floor at the foot of the bed. Still wearing an overcoat and galoshes, the body "lay curled upon the floor." Astrid was lying on the bed, with a revolver in her limp right hand. She had apparently shot herself in the head after killing Vestal. The fatal bullet had gone through his heart and out his back; it was found in the folds of his coat.

Although she was still alive when she was first found, Astrid died shortly afterward without saying anything. It appeared to the police, who were called by Dr. Barton, that Astrid's first shot missed LeRoy because a bullet was found embedded in a wall behind where he had most likely been standing. Her second shot killed him. She directed a third shot to her own head.

Police found a purse on a table in the room. It contained a short note and $430 in cash. She wrote that "if anything happens to me, please send word" to her thirteen-year-old son in Norway. She asked for the money to be sent to him also.

Vestal still had his coat on, but he had removed his hat and gloves. Given the gap in time between his arrival and the shots, the couple likely had a conversation. Police conjectured that Astrid had hidden the gun in the bedclothes before pulling it out to kill Vestal.

What occurred during that conversation? We will never know, but we can certainly speculate. Perhaps the most likely explanation is that Astrid had become pregnant with LeRoy's child. In all likelihood, an earlier unplanned pregnancy had resulted in his marriage to Nadja, and Astrid had left another child behind in Norway; a second one outside of marriage would have been unwelcomed by either one.

Although the murder-suicide merited front-page coverage in the newspaper, there was no written speculation about a motive. The newspaper simply noted the couple had "been friendly," without any details. It was unlikely there was an autopsy since the cause of death was evident – her death certificate notes it was caused by a gunshot.

Somewhat ironically, the gun that killed Vestal had been a Christmas gift in a previous time from Astrid's then-husband, Stephen Crowell. He continued to be close enough to his ex-wife that he provided the information for her death certificate and signed it as providing that information.

Both Astrid Crowell and LeRoy Vestal are buried in Juneau's Evergreen Cemetery; LeRoy in the American Legion section. Astrid Crowell's grave is unmarked.

After her ex-husband's death, Nadja continued to be close to her in-laws, and still traveled with Mrs. Day occasionally. She also remained active on the social scene and remarried. In July 1936, the newspaper noted that she and three other people were stranded on Shelter Island near Juneau for two days due to bad weather. Those accompanying her were Mr. and Mrs. W. Triplette and Hollis Triplette. Three years after that incident, she married Hollis, known familiarly as Holly, in a "quiet ceremony." Holly Triplette worked in the mechanical office of the newspaper.

Nadja Triplette died in 1972 at age seventy; her husband, Holly, lived four years longer, dying in 1976 at age sixty-nine. The couple is buried next to each other in Juneau's Evergreen Cemetery.

Two years after the murder-suicide, Astrid's ex-husband, Stephen Crowell, moved to Honolulu, where he spent the rest of his long life, dying at age eighty-four in Kahului on the island of Maui. He had also remarried, to a Japanese woman fifteen years his junior, Meiko. The couple had four children.

Perhaps the saddest part of this tragic story happened after LeRoy's death. Leroy Jr. had the high school experience that his father had missed by enlisting. LeRoy Jr. was active in Boy Scouts and involved in both school and community activities. In March 1941, his grandmother, Mrs. Day, gave him an eighteenth birthday party. A month later, in April 1941, he was among the students who performed a patriotic concert in Juneau. He graduated that May, and in the fall, went to Pullman, WA to attend Washington State University. He returned after his first year of college in spring 1942 to spend the summer in Juneau. In October, he was drafted, ten months after the Japanese attack on Pearl Harbor. Leroy began his service in the Alaska Territorial Guard in Juneau. His first service out of Juneau was in the Aleutian islands, which the Japanese attacked in June 1942.

After becoming a corporal and entering the regular army, Leroy joined the infantry and was first sent to Hawaii and then to the Marshall Islands. The Marshalls were considered prime locations for airfields and other support operations for anticipated American battles in the Pacific against the Japanese. On the last day of the battle for the islands, which the U.S. won, Leroy was killed, one of 611 American soldiers who died. He was twenty years old. He is buried next to his father in the American Legion portion of Evergreen Cemetery.

Chapter 8: The Cookie Jar Murder

The shooting death of a forty-four-year-old steamship cook in Juneau in 1938 prompted the local newspaper to assign enough nicknames to the killing for a handful of murders. The death of Thomas Colling was called the "salad dressing" slaying, the "cookie jar" murder, and the "Red Bat" killing. In one notable article, it was called "the salad dressing, cookie jar triangle case." The case itself could be considered fairly simple – a husband killed his wife's boyfriend. But it was complicated by the killer's intricate efforts to set up the shooting.

Forrest Victor Smith was a painter at the Alaska Juneau Gold Mine, a going concern in 1938. Perched on the mountainside above downtown Juneau, it employed about one thousand people and was the main commercial enterprise in town. Smith had been working there since July 1928 and may have come to Juneau to take the job.

In October 1938, Smith's wife, Thelma, asked him for a divorce. He asked her to wait for five days, so he could spend more time with their daughter. Instead, he used the time to put in motion an elaborate plan to kill his wife's friend, Thomas Colling, (and possibly his wife).

The deception started when Smith told Thelma he was planning a three-day trip to visit some mining claims near Juneau. He timed his alleged departure with the day of the arrival of the steamship that employed Colling. After supposedly leaving to go on the trip, he hired a taxi cab driver to drive up to his house on Gastineau Avenue in downtown Juneau. He told the cabbie that his wife didn't want him to go hunting, so he needed to sneak into the house's basement to grab his gun. The cabbie agreed, for a fee, to distract Smith's wife while Smith went into the basement, which had a separate entrance.

The cab driver dropped Smith off a distance from the house, and then the driver drove to the house pretending to be seeking someone else as his excuse to engage Mrs. Smith in conversation. After a brief time, the cab driver left, as Smith had requested.

While Thelma talked to the cab driver, Smith ducked into the house's basement, where he had set up a cot and

JUNEAUITE HELD AFTER SHOOTING WIFE'S "LOVER"

Smith Bond Fixed at $10,-000 After Coroner's Jury Brings in Verdict

WIFE ADMITS SENDING LOVE NOTE TO STEWARD

Tale of Shattered Romance, Alleged Illicit Relations Told on Stand

Headline from *Alaska Daily Empire* Oct. 13, 1938

supplies to allow him to lie in wait for Colling's ship to arrive. (Steamships were often late, which is why the prosecution at the later trial said Smith had set up a cot and food in case he had to wait longer than a day.)

Thelma and Forrest Smith had been married just four years, tying the knot in Juneau in May 1934. The marriage certificate notes that Smith was a laborer living in Juneau; his bride, Thelma Archambault, had moved to Alaska to sell lingerie at a Juneau department store earlier that year. He stated that he was forty years old and that she was twenty-five. Three years later, their daughter, Louise, was born.

Forrest Smith was not actually "Forrest Smith"; his real name was Jesse Orville Bonsall, and he was born in Missouri on June 16, 1892. This fact came out a day after the shooting, during the hearing before the coroner's jury. Apparently, the district attorney's office had uncovered his alias before the hearing. Smith, however, confessed only "that he was not sure of his true name but that he believed it was Bonsall."

After that one brief mention, the matter never came up again in newspaper coverage, and he continued to be called Smith. According to federal files, however, he was known to have several aliases, including Victor Foster, Jack Smith, F.V. Smith, and Darien Smith. It appears that Smith is one of the men who came to Alaska to escape his past; a

Photo of Colling from unnamed true crime magazine article. *Courtesy of Alaska State Historic Archives.*

move that was common then and not unheard of today.

The course toward murder began in 1938, when Thelma took a steamship south with her nine-month-old baby; her husband said it was to seek dental care. She would also have visited her parents, who lived in Seattle. It is likely that she met Colling on that trip south. He was a cook aboard the steamship *Tongass*.

Colling had spent several years in northern Alaska, where he met his wife, Jeanette Belles, a nurse in Nenana and his senior by about ten years. The couple married in 1921, according to the Nenana Daily News.

It noted that both bride and groom "are well and favorably known in Nenana. The bride is a member of the nursing staff at the Government Hospital, having arrived from the States on one of the last boats last fall to make her residence in Nenana. The groom is an oldtimer of the North." In that period of time, an "oldtimer" didn't refer to the person's age as much as an extended stay in the area. And extended stay could be any time more than three or four years.

The couple had a baby boy two years later, according to the newspaper. But the child apparently didn't survive, since Mrs. Colling was reported as living with only their daughter, age thirteen, in 1938 in Seattle. The couple also appeared to have drifted apart; the 1930 census shows Mrs. Colling and her daughter living with her sister and brother-in-law in Seattle. Thomas Colling was not part of the household.

But in September 1938, Thomas Colling was working aboard the *Tongass* when Thelma and her now one-year-old daughter boarded the steamship for their return trip to Juneau. At the time, most people coming in and out of Alaska traveled via steamship. The ships plied the waters on a regular schedule between Seattle and Alaska ports. Then, as now, Alaska ship crews would often live in Seattle, but some also chose to live in the Alaska ports where they regularly docked. According to Mrs. Colling, she and her husband were living together at the time of his slaying. (A fellow crew member on the *Tongass*, however, said that he thought that Colling was living apart from his wife.)

During this trip, witnesses said the cook and the new mother seemed to have a long-standing relationship. The witnesses, another Juneau woman and a crewmate of Colling's, later testified that the two were often in each other's company. The crewmate, the ship's purser, testified that he had seen Mrs. Smith leave Colling's room at 11:00 p.m. one night. "They acted as if they had known each other for a long time, and I supposed they had," he said.

"If she wasn't in his stateroom, he was in her's or they were around together somewhere else," a fellow passenger, Mrs. Christine Zinck, later testified. Mrs. Zinck described watching the sleeping baby Louise one night while the boat was docked in Ketchikan. She said that she had been asked to watch the baby while Colling and Thelma Smith went to a dance but that they didn't return until 4:00 a.m. and Mrs. Smith had been drinking. This was during prohibition, so Mrs. Smith's drinking broke the law. It was a common crime, and often no charges were filed. Mrs. Zinck also said she had seen Colling leaving Mrs. Smith's stateroom while wearing his pajamas.

Once back in Juneau, Mrs. Zinck wasn't shy about sharing her suspicions, and word soon reached Smith that his wife had been indiscreet with a crew member of the *Tongass*. Smith contacted Mrs. Zinck and asked her for more details which she readily provided.

Very soon after returning to Juneau on Sept. 17, Mrs. Smith told her husband she wanted a divorce. (Her husband later testified she asked for the divorce "as quick as she got off the boat.") She said she wanted the divorce by Oct. 15. Smith responded by saying he wanted more time with his daughter and asked to postpone filing for divorce until Oct. 20. He then put his plan into action.

In addition to setting up temporary quarters in the basement, Smith paid a friend a dollar to rent his gun, saying he might use it to shoot grouse. He also arranged for another friend to talk to Thelma about the fictitious hunting trip to convince her it was genuine.

In the basement of his own home, Smith waited for the sound of Colling coming into the house. He was sitting below the kitchen and later testified that he listened to Colling and his wife for some period before going outside the basement, which was accessed only through an outside door and entering the kitchen door of the house.

He said he opened the door and saw his wife sitting on a man's lap as they embraced. He later testified:

"As quick as they saw me, Mrs. Smith jumped up and Colling came charging at me like a football player. I shouted to him to stop or he would get killed, but when he came on and grabbed me around the legs, I shot. He then pushed me back over a table and I shot again but about that time, he crumbled up on the floor. I felt his pulse, saw he was dead, called the ambulance and then the authorities."

Although Smith called police immediately, it took some time before he was arrested. He killed Colling on Oct. 13, but wasn't charged until the next day, after the coroner's jury met. The U.S. Commissioner in Juneau, who oversaw the district attorney and federal marshal's offices, had asked the coroner's jury to determine whether the shooting was in self-defense. It declined to do so, and Assistant District Attorney George Folta, who was assigned to prosecute the case, then filed manslaughter charges against Smith, and he was arrested.

The coroner's jury also heard from Mrs. Smith, who was described by the newspaper's reporter. "Mrs. Smith, a woman of 30, wearing horned rimmed glasses, a large red hat and visibly shaken, denied her husband had cause to shoot Colling."

Her story of the shooting was markedly different from her husband's.

She said Colling had come by the house to bring her a jar from the ship that she had told him she would like to use for salad dressing. When he arrived with the jar, he had filled it with homemade cookies. She said she pulled out one to eat.

"I asked Mr. Colling if he wanted one and he said no, he preferred to smoke. So, I was eating my cookie standing by the radio and Mr. Colling was sitting in the chair smoking when Jack (she referred to her husband as Jack) opened the door. He just burst in shooting." She added that Smith said, "I've caught you this time, or something like that and started shooting."

She denied she was sitting on Colling's lap and emphasized that Colling had no time to respond to Smith's arrival and did not attack him. The physician who examined Colling's body said the one bullet that entered his body was shot at an angle, as if fired from above. The bullet's path could have resulted from either being shot while sitting or while tackling Smith's legs. Smith said he had put a bullet in the 22 pistol's chamber as they entered the room. The first shot missed Colling completely, but the second hit his heart.

As the newspaper described Smith's behavior and the shooting, it also gave front-page coverage to the letter that prompted the unlikely nickname of "Red Bat" to the killing. The letter, which was found in the dead man's possession, had been delivered by a cab driver to Colling's steamship the day the ship docked in Juneau. Signed by "Red Bat," Thelma Smith admitted to the coroner's jury that she had written it. It was printed in its entirety in the *Daily Alaska Empire* of Juneau.

Although presented in ensuing court proceedings as a love letter, it reads in part as a desperate plea from a lonely woman.

"Dearest Tom,

Oh how I've been waiting for you to come back to me, so I can hold you again near to me. It seems years since I've seen you, and am just waiting till I can be with you.

Mrs. Thomas Colling, widow of the seaman murdered in love nest tryst, and her pretty daughter Jeannette.

Photo of Colling's wife and daughter from unnamed true crime magazine article. Courtesy of Alaska State Historic Archives.

I'm sending this by cab driver as I've been unable to get down to Fommers.

Tonite's latest report on the *Tongass* is that you'll get in at 8 a.m.

Now I must tell you "Our" good luck. The A.J. has taken over the Claims Jack lost thru not keeping up the assessment work [she's referring to mining claims made by her husband that were now claimed by the Alaska Juneau gold mine]. And as he staked all that property he has been hired to go and re-stake them with 3 other men. He's to be gone from Juneau till Sat. AM sometime. He is now on Graveyard shift 11 PM to 6:45 AM. Taking a hot bath. Eating a big breakfast. Wearing his hunting clothes & leaving here by taxi to Thane and from there going on the trail to Grindstone Creek where the other 3 men are with a boat. So Tom I'm telling you all this so you have some idea what he's all about. Now you know how long the *Tongass* will be here and I want to see you all the time I can, that you can spare me.

Oh I've so much to tell you – just wish you were here now.

Little Louise has been very sick with a cold but Thank God she's better but I can't leave her, and I was wondering if you would come to me? I'll be patiently waiting for you. I do wish you'd send me word by cab driver or come up. Now I don't know the exact hour Jack will leave but imagine he won't stay here longer than 9:30 or 10 AM but I don't know. I know you have your lunch to get but thought if you could come up we could talk a little anyway. If you can't come up till afternoon or Evening would you send up a note to let me know "when" I can look for you as I'll be counting the minutes till I can see you. If you did send up a note & Jack was here it wouldn't make any real trouble if you sign "Mrs. Zinck's" name I'll know but I'm positive he'll be away from here by at least 9:30 AM that gives him 3 hrs here and it can't take him any longer. I know this is on the Square as Sam Ducker (lawyer) came here to the house and they made the deal as he went over to his office yesterday at 1:30 PM to settle everything.

Gee I could write pages tonight to you, there I go again "Bothering" you but you've been so swell to me I can't understand what you can see in me, all I do is cry around on your shoulder but Tom I need you so much as I've gone thru so much since I've seen you, and the old fight I was going to muster up has just about been swallowed up by tears. I guess I'm a coward or yellow or whatever you want to call it; anyhow if I didn't have Louise & you to look forward to ... I'm afraid there just wouldn't be a "Me" but I've hung on and that's why I want to see you as soon as I can as I feel I'll go stark mad if I can't find someone who doesn't tell me I'm everything from the lowest thing down. So please try & come or let me know your Plans or send me word as I'll be watching out my windows at the old *Tongass* & imagining just what you are doing.

Love, Red Bat"

The nickname Red Bat was later described by Thelma as referring to a joke that she and Colling had seen during a stop in the Southeast Alaska town of Petersburg – a local man would show people something he called a "red bat." It was a brick in a cardboard box.

Smith had obviously planned to seek a self-defense determination; it is likely his arrest was delayed because the police and federal marshals expected the coroner's jury to reach that conclusion. After all, Smith shot a strange man in his own house. Self-defense would have been an obvious conclusion.

But the coroner's jury in Smith's case saw something other than self-defense. Its members saw a man holed up in his own basement waiting for his wife's boyfriend to show up so he could surprise and kill him. This was not a case of self-defense; instead, it seemed like premeditated murder. Smith was indicted for first-degree murder by a grand jury in mid-November. His trial was scheduled for early December, less than seven weeks following the killing.

This speed occurred despite the newspaper noting that at the time of the grand jury hearing, Smith still didn't have an attorney. He ended up being assigned two attorneys on Nov. 21 -- George Grigsby and Paul Danzig. Grigsby had a noteworthy political resume; he had served as Alaska's delegate to the U.S. House of Representatives for one year and was Alaska's attorney general for three years during its first years as a territory. (He was also the defendant's attorney in the Ketchikan case of 1931 described earlier in this book.) In 1938, Grigsby was sixty-four, and his age may have prompted the judge to assign a second attorney. The younger Danzig had lived in Juneau about a year before being named to represent Smith. He lived there only briefly before moving to Seward.

Surprisingly, a third attorney was appointed by Judge George Alexander when the case went to trial on Dec. 1. Henry Roden, who also had a political resume as a senator in the Alaska Territorial Legislature, was added to the defense table. Roden was to become Attorney General just two years later and ultimately served as the Territorial Treasurer shortly before statehood. Assistant District Attorney George Folta continued to be assigned as prosecutor.

Seating the jury was a time-consuming process, involving calling forty-nine potential jurors. Many were disqualified because they knew either the defendant, the victim, or a witness. Others were challenged by questions regarding what the newspaper referred to as "the unwritten law." That apparently referred to the idea that a man killing his wife's lover in his home was always justified.

The prosecution case took just half a day. It relied primarily on testimony from the deputy federal marshal, Walter Hellan, who had been called to the scene of the crime. Hellan described finding Smith sitting in his living room. Smith told him of waiting in the basement for four hours before hearing Colling and coming to the kitchen door. The body was still on the floor in the kitchen.

After the prosecution rested on Friday, Dec. 2, the judge recessed the trial until the following Monday to give the defense two more days to prepare.

Facing a defendant who admitted to planning and executing the murder, the trio of defense attorneys chose the somewhat risky defense of claiming insanity.

Smith wasn't pleased. He twice told the judge he didn't want to claim insanity, but it was to no avail. He also argued with his lawyers about whether he would testify. Initially, he planned to testify but raised enough questions about it for the judge to give him thirty minutes to reconsider. He ultimately decided not to take the stand.

The defense brought in two witnesses who described the elaborate (and unconvincing) lies they had been told in the past by Smith. Charles Carter told the crowded courtroom that he became a close friend of Smith in 1929. During their five years of friendship, Carter testified that he heard so many fantastical stories from Smith that he initially believed the man was insane. Later, he decided that Smith was just a liar, Carter told the court.

He said Smith told him he descended from British nobility and was related to high-ranking officials of the British armed forces. Another friend, Arley Mullins, testified that Smith told him he worked for the Federal Bureau of Narcotics and was in Juneau "trying to clean up the traffic in dope." Mullins added that Smith told him that about ten years previously, which didn't lend much credibility to the insanity defense.

There was also an attempt by the defense to admit the "Red Bat" letter as a motivation in Smith's actions. Since, however, Smith had not seen it until it was presented to the coroner's jury, the judge didn't allow it to be used.

On the third day of the trial and second day of defense witnesses, Smith again refused to testify and again complained about the insanity defense proposed by his attorneys. The newspaper noted that he declared "that he had told his story to Assistant District Attorney George Folta and the prosecutor had treated him fairly. He stressed that there was no other story to tell."

The star witness this day was Christine Zinck, the Juneau resident and passenger on the *Tongass* who had watched the one-year-old Louise Smith when Thelma Smith went ashore in Ketchikan with Tom Colling. She repeated the testimony she had given the coroner's jury about the couple in each other's rooms and Thelma Smith returning to the steamship inebriated.

On the following day, Wednesday, Dec. 7, the case went to the jury at about 2:30 p.m. And that's where it stayed. On the 8th, the jury asked to see the scene of the crime and its members were taken to the Smiths' house on Gastineau Avenue. They had been charged by the judge with deciding among first-degree murder calling for capital punishment, first-degree murder and a lifetime prison sentence, second-degree murder, manslaughter, and acquittal.

On Saturday at about 10:00 p.m., the jurors told the judge they were deadlocked, and he dismissed them. The newspaper reported that the jurors had voted ten to two to convict. It further noted that six wanted a manslaughter conviction, four voted for first-degree murder and two wanted to acquit. Prosecutor George Folta immediately announced the case would be retried.

Thelma Archambault as a high school senior.

And it was, again with dizzying speed. The second trial began on Jan. 24, just six weeks after the first trial ended. There was trouble selecting a jury; this time, nearly one hundred potential jurors were questioned before a full jury was seated. It consisted of ten men and two women; the first jury was composed of seven women and five men.

This time, however, Assistant District Attorney George Folta added a witness – Thelma Smith. Wearing a dark coat and hat, Thelma told the courtroom – again packed with local residents curious about the case – that her relationship with Colling was platonic. "Mr. Colling treated me as a decent woman. He was someone I could talk to. He was just a friend."

Because she was on the witness stand, the defense attorneys succeeded in introducing the "Red Bat" letter. Thelma Smith described the shooting. The newspaper wrote that she said that the couple was in the living room when her husband entered the room from the kitchen.

"He [Colling] had taken a seat near the radio and I came in and sat down across the room from him. I had just taken a bite of my cookie when I heard a noise and jumped up. My husband was standing in the doorway with a gun in his hand.

"He said, 'I've been laying for you and I'm going to kill you,' and Mr. Colling jumped up – and they started struggling for the gun back through the kitchen door into the kitchen.

"I was near the front room door – I don't know what I was doing, and I heard a shot – then I heard another shot.

"Jack came out of the kitchen then with the gun and said 'Get down on your knees or I'll kill you.'

"I said, 'Go ahead, Jack, shoot me,' but he said, 'No, you stay here,' and then he left – to call the police, I guess."

Perhaps the strangest part of this odd case came at the end of her testimony, when Judge Alexander (the same judge from the previous trial) allowed the defendant to cross-examine his wife.

The questions Smith asked appeared inconsequential; he asked about a note she had found and the number of cigarettes she had smoked on the day of the killing. In one exchange, he also took the opportunity to accuse her of leaving their baby girl alone in the house while she went to a beer parlor, and of changing her testimony in court from what she gave at the coroner's inquest. The judge twice asked him to move on and finally told him to stop the cross-examination.

One of the most interesting exchanges came when Thelma Smith was asked by prosecutor Folta why she wanted a divorce.

She replied, "I found out a lot of lies about him when I was Outside [Alaska]. I found he owed a lot of bills he said he had paid, that I was his third wife, that the baby was his fourth child, and that Smith was not even his right name." Grigsby objected to this testimony, and the judge told the jury to disregard it.

At the end of the day, the newspaper reporter described Smith as "well-groomed in a dark suit and for the greater part of the proceedings, sat with a cigarette in a long cigarette holder, smoking calmly and unruffled."

MORE FORGOTTEN MURDERS FROM ALASKA   121

Despite her criticism of her husband, when the defense began its case the following day, attorney Grigsby called Mrs. Smith's testimony "a magnificent present" to the defense. He claimed that Thelma was "testifying for her lover – she was prompted to coming to the stand with her stories by a motive of revenge – and she wants to see her husband in the penitentiary."

The earlier defense of insanity doesn't appear to have been brought up in the second trial. In fact, it appears that Grigsby and Danzig (Roden isn't mentioned in newspaper coverage of this trial) instead relied on attacking Thelma Smith during their closing argument. Grigsby referred to the "unwritten law," stating that a man's home is his castle and accusing Thelma of lying about not being on Colling's lap or having intimate relations with him.

Danzig accused Colling of breaking up Smith's family and, with Thelma, setting "off a chain of circumstances which places Smith before you today."

Prosecutor Folta then told the jury that Smith "murdered in revenge without legal defense" and suggested that Thelma's testimony indicated that Smith also meant to shoot his wife. He said, "There was hatred and murder in his mind when he made her get down on her knees, but when she said, 'Go ahead, Jack, shoot me,' he couldn't go through with it."

The jury deliberated on the third day of the trial, Jan. 26, 1939. In instructing the jury, Judge Alexander told them there was no such thing as an "unwritten law" and it played no part in the case. The jury met until it reached a verdict at 2:00 a.m. the next day.

Forrest Smith was convicted of second-degree murder; the jury members also asked for a lenient sentence. At the time, such a conviction required a sentence of at least fifteen years, according to the newspaper.

On Feb. 4, about a week later, Judge Alexander sentenced Forrest, along with a handful of other people convicted of lesser crimes. Smith received twenty years to be served at McNeil Island Federal Penitentiary in Washington State.

When Thelma Smith received the word of her husband's conviction, she was feeding her daughter at a local restaurant. According to the newspaper, "She said she had no comment and had no definite plans."

But within a few days (one day before Smith was sentenced to twenty years), the newspaper noted that Thelma had filed for divorce, on the grounds of his murder conviction. She was granted the divorce within a year, in 1939, and in September 1940, she was married again, to Fred Harold Folette. Folette had not lived in Juneau long before he married Thelma. It appeared he adopted Louise, who took his name. In 1950, the couple purchased a house in Douglas, but just a year later, Fred Folette, who had a janitorial service, died at age forty-three. He is buried at Evergreen Cemetery in Juneau.

Thelma, widowed, married a third time in September 1954. Now forty-six years old, she married a fisherman ten years her senior, Thomas W. Peterson. Peterson was from Elfin Cove, a tiny fishing village about seventy air miles from Juneau.

And it was in Elfin Cove where Thelma herself passed away in 1999, at age ninety. It appears that her daughter, Louise Mourant (she married Robert Mourant in 1957), was with her. Louise died eleven years later in 2010, at age seventy-two. Thelma's third husband, "Pete" Peterson, had died twenty-five years earlier in 1978. The Petersons rest together at a cemetery in Snohomish, WA.

At some point, the Bonsall family learned what had happened to Jesse Orville Bonsall, who had been born on June 16, 1892, in Missouri. Bonsall, who was known as Forrest Smith in Juneau, had been married twice before he wed Thelma, just as Thelma had told the jury. In 1915, at age twenty-three, he married Beatrice May Hardy in Washington State. The couple had two daughters and a son over the next three years. It appears that Bonsall, who was known by that name at the time, was working in Chelan, WA as a fruit farmer.

In 1928, when his second daughter, Ada, was eleven years old, she died. That same year, he left his family and moved to Juneau as

Forrest Smith. There, he married Lavina Mae Carter in 1930; the couple had one daughter, Sarah, the following year. Just three years after his daughter was born, he married again, this time to Thelma.

Why did he change his name? It may be because he had not divorced Beatrice before leaving Washington. That would mean both his marriages in Juneau were bigamous. His daughter by Lavina, Sarah, grew up in Juneau. Her mother lived all her life in Juneau and remarried after supposedly divorcing Forrest Smith. What is puzzling now is why she and her daughter were never mentioned in the news coverage about Colling's murder. Perhaps it's because Lavina had remarried in 1936, two years before the murder, so she had both a new last name and husband.

Jesse Orville Bonsall, aka Forrest Smith, died in 1967 at age seventy-five. He served at least twelve years since the 1950 census puts him still in McNeil Federal Penitentiary.

Chapter 9: The Fourth Husband

It was late on a Monday night in October 1946 when Juneau police officer John Homme responded to a call about an injured man at a home in downtown Juneau. Homme may have responded to previous calls at that same property; it was a boarding house after all. He may even have responded to other calls from the caller and landlady, Clara Andrews, since it was not the first time she had been beaten by her husband, Ralph Andrews.

The patrolman found Clara bruised and bloody in the couple's bedroom. On the floor was the dented metal trash can her husband had beaten her with. Her tall, two-hundred-pound husband was also in bad shape, bleeding profusely from a head wound. Clara readily admitted what had happened while she used a towel to staunch her husband's wound.

She said that Ralph was drunk and angry and attacked her while she lay in bed. Ralph had hit her on the head, jaw, chest, and legs with the metal trash can. She said she seized the first thing she could grab – a glass of water on the bedside table – and flung it at her husband's head. The glass broke in two, cutting him significantly. Ralph stopped beating her, but he didn't stop bleeding, and now Clara was worried.

Clara called a doctor, William Blanton, who found Ralph sitting up in bed, "smiling sheepishly," the doctor would later testify. The doctor examined Ralph and decided he wasn't critically injured. Because the bleeding was not stopping, however, the doctor called for an ambulance to St. Ann's Hospital, just a few blocks from the house.

At the hospital, the doctor stitched up a two-inch cut on Ralph's head. Dr. Blanton had a history with Ralph Andrews, which may be

THE DAILY ALASKA EMPIRE — JUNEAU, ALASKA

In Juneau Tragedy

Mr. and Mrs. Andrews shortly after their marriage.
The photo appeared in the *Alaska Daily Empire*.

why he decided he didn't need to anesthetize him before stitching the wound, and why he easily admitted "he had done absolutely nothing" about the injury at the house. Blanton later claimed that Andrews was "so drunk" that he didn't need a painkiller. He also testified that Andrews seemed unbothered by his injury and "didn't appear to be paying the least attention to it."

Initially, at the hospital, Dr. Blanton said Ralph's blood pressure was good, a sign that the injury wasn't critical. Suddenly it plummeted, indicating internal bleeding. The doctor said he tried to inject plasma to boost blood volume but was unsuccessful.

And so, an hour and forty minutes after he was hit on his temple with a water glass, Ralph Andrews died. An autopsy conducted the following evening stated that he had gone into shock from loss of blood.

Somewhat surprisingly, Clara Andrews was quickly arrested and charged with second-degree murder. The district attorney who called for her arrest, Robert Boochever, was new to the job, and may have been trying to make a name for himself, as the case seemed to be more self-defense than murder. There was also some precedent set in Juneau for women not being charged with murder after demonstrating a history of abuse. As early as 1916 in Juneau, a young housemaid had shot her husband while he tried to strangle her and was not indicted after the coroner's jury determined she acted in self-defense.

It's possible that the attention paid to the death may have put some additional pressure on Assistant District Attorney Boochever. On Nov. 5, 1946, *Daily Alaska Empire* readers saw an all-caps, banner headline proclaiming Mrs. Andrews had slain her husband, Ralph, by striking him on the temple with a water glass. The top of the page read, "MAN KILLED BY FATAL BLOW ON TEMPLE" in large type. A secondary headline said, "WIFE HITS R. ANDREWS FATAL BLOW" and, in smaller type, "TRAGEDY OCCURS IN GOLD STREET EARLY THIS MORNING."

Another murder case less than a week before may have also played a role in Boochever's decision. On Oct. 30, six days before the glass was thrown at Ralph Andrew's temple, an elderly man shot a stranger in his house in downtown Juneau. Thomas Ashby, eighty-one, killed a man who was bringing home Ashby's inebriated son. The son was too drunk to make his way home unassisted, so Stanley Hanning offered to help him home. The homeowner saw Hanning, who he did not know, as a threat and killed him. The shooter, Ashby, claimed self-defense but was quickly indicted on first-degree murder.

THE DAILY ALASKA EMPIRE

"ALL THE NEWS ALL THE TIME"

VOL. LXVIII, NO. 10,418   JUNEAU, ALASKA, TUESDAY, NOVEMBER 5, 1946   MEMBER ASSOCIATED PRESS   PRICE TEN CENTS

MAN KILLED BY FATAL BLOW ON TEMPLE

The *Alaska Daily Empire's* banner headline after Mr. Andrews' death, published Nov. 5, 1946.

For Boochever to then be presented with another killer claiming self-defense may have been a bridge too far for the twenty-one-year-old inexperienced prosecutor. This was Boochever's first legal job since graduating from Cornell University in 1939. After law school, he joined the Army and served in WWII, getting out in 1945.

Thomas Ashby was able to eventually win his case based on self-defense, with the court agreeing Ashby felt his home was being threatened at the time of the shooting, but Boochever wouldn't learn that until more than a year later. Now, he was faced with another defendant who claimed to have been a victim, not just a killer. Fortunately for Clara Andrews, the evidence supported her claim.

Ralph Andrew's death came at a time of great change in Juneau. The gold mines that drove the city's economy for sixty years had recently closed. By the early 1940s, the Alaska-Juneau Gold Mine, right next to a growing downtown, had produced about 3.5 million ounces of gold and about half that weight in silver. In 2025 prices, the bullion would have been worth nearly $250 billion.

But by 1944, production had dropped significantly. On April 10, mine operators announced the mine would close at midnight, the end of the second shift, because profits were too low. Around 250 miners lost their jobs. Ore processing was too expensive, and World War II had drained the mine's workforce, which was usually around 1,000. The A-J was the final Alaska mine to close. Federal officials had shut down most others to provide workers for war industries.

Despite the shutdown, Juneau's population was growing in the 1940s. It had been 5,700 in 1940 and grew to almost 6,000 in 1950.

That's because soldiers returned from the battlefields and workers from wartime industries settled down and started having children.

Ralph Andrews had not been in Clara's life for long. So, who was he? It's a little hard to tell from records because he had a common name. However, he appears to have moved to Alaska from Washington state, where a Ralph Andrews is listed in multiple public records as being born in 1901 in Aberdeen, about fifty miles west of the capital of Olympia. The 1920 census appears to list the same person, a nineteen-year-old soldier, assigned to a base near San Antonio, Texas.

That Ralph Andrews married a woman named Juanita Jones in 1922 in Olympia, though the relationship didn't last. He had at least one run-in with the law in 1926. He was arrested and charged with possession of liquor during prohibition. He paid a fine and was released. Such a charge was common at the time. We next hear from Andrews in 1942, when he registered for the draft in his hometown of Aberdeen. Two years later, steamship passenger lists published in Juneau's newspaper show him arriving from Seattle at the age of forty-three.

In Juneau, Andrews was "employed intermittently as a cook in various local restaurants and hotels" according to newspaper reports. A 1946 advertisement announced he had been hired as the new chef at the Gastineau Café. Gastineau was a common business name, taken from Gastineau Channel, the ocean passage separating Juneau from the nearby town of Douglas. Ralph met Clara at the Bus Depot Café where she washed dishes.

In addition to being charged with murder, Clara Andrews again found herself a widow. She had liked getting married. She just didn't have much luck staying that way. By that fateful night in 1946, at the age of fifty-three, she had tied the knot four times.

Clara Marie Berthold was born Dec. 22, 1893 in New York City. Her parents were German immigrants and had one other child, also a daughter. Clara attended school through the eighth grade.

In 1923, at the age of thirty, she married her first husband, Frederick Effler, a German immigrant and jeweler, in Manhattan.

She may have met the forty-six-year-old at the store where she was clerking. They had no children together.

Six years after marrying Effler, Clara left him and came to Alaska. Her first stop was Wrangell, an island city of about nine-hundred people 150 miles southeast of Juneau. The Wrangell Sentinel newspaper wrote that she arrived on the Steamship Alameda at the end of November 1929. It listed her previous residence as in West Virginia, which was almost certainly untrue.

The newspaper wrote the relative she stayed with was her sister, Verna Morke, whose husband, Edward, owned the Wrangell Sanitary Dairy. But census and other records show Clara had only one sister, Theresa, who never left the East Coast. Perhaps Verna was a cousin or simply a friend. Records show she was from Chehalis, Washington, and her last name was Collins before she married Edward.

A year and a half after she moved to Wrangell, Clara married August Romansuth (Royomunseth in court papers), a Norwegian who captained a cannery tender. Such ships brought salmon from fish traps or fishing boats to processing plants where they were canned and then shipped south for sale. Clara and August were wed on March 25, 1931, in Juneau. He was forty-nine and she was thirty-nine. The newspaper reported Clara was from Colorado Springs, Colorado, though she had been living in Wrangell.

The differing stories of her home – Colorado or West Virginia – may have been Clara's attempt to mask her real home of Manhattan, where she left her first husband. He was likely still her legal husband. Her 1931 marriage license listed Frederick as deceased, but he wasn't. Documents from New York indicate that he didn't die until 1937. At the time, Alaska was a place where people went to reinvent themselves. Well-known Alaska artist Sydney Laurence was among the many people who left a spouse behind for the distant territory. Like Laurence, Clara must have decided (correctly) that no one would discover the truth of her bigamy.

A Wrangell friend attended the March wedding, and the newspaper again listed her as a sister. The "sister" was now named

Mrs. A. Kramer, which may have been a newspaper error or the name that Verna was using at the time – just a few years before her own divorce. Clara's groom appears to have left his first wife, Petra, as well as their two children, to marry Clara. There may have been love at first, but the marriage didn't last much more than two years. Clara sued for divorce in early April of 1933, saying August beat her.

Court documents related to her filing for divorce say that in 1932 he struck and bruised her, later slapping her so hard she fell against a sideboard and was injured. The following year, he restrained her while his son Joe beat her. A month later, August threatened to fix her "so that no other man could have her."

The testimony was part of a trial before a judge, not a jury. That judge determined that August had, for more than a year, "treated (Clara) in a cruel and inhuman manner such as is calculated to impair her health and endanger her life." He wrote she was justified in fearing her husband "will either kill or seriously injure her."

On the day the judge granted Clara the divorce, August wasn't in the courtroom, according to court records. His attorney was his representative. The judge also granted Clara her request to resume using the name Effler, which he belived was her maiden name.

August moved to Washington state in 1946, where he remarried, this time to Gertrude Olsen, the following year. That marriage didn't last long either. August Romansuth died in 1948.

Clara didn't use the name Effler for long, just until she married eighteen months after the divorce, in November 1933. She was wed this time to Alexander Zibio, an Alaska-Juneau Gold Mine worker and Austrian immigrant. Zibio was forty-five and she was forty. He had two years of college, which was uncommon for an industrial worker at the time.

They had several good years together, buying a home on Gold Street in downtown Juneau shortly after the wedding. Then, Zibio was diagnosed with tuberculosis, which killed him three years later at Juneau's St. Ann's Hospital at the age of fifty-six. He was buried in the city cemetery. Clara cared for him as his health failed and was never suspected of any wrongdoing. At some point, she turned their home into a boarding house, which she was running in 1945.

In addition to running the boarding house, Clara was also washing dishes at the Bus Depot Café, where she probably met Ralph Anderson. He had been working as a cook in several downtown Juneau restaurants and cafes. Clara married her fourth husband Ralph Andrews on Oct. 13, 1945, when she was fifty-two and he was forty-five. After his death, the newspaper printed a photo of the couple taken after their marriage. It is not a portrait of a happy couple.

One problem was that Ralph liked to drink too much and had a drug problem. In fact, in May of 1946, he was charged with eleven federal felony counts for obtaining narcotics by fraud or deceit in Juneau. U.S. Marshalls alleged he purchased morphine tablets, a commonly prescribed painkiller, using the name of Roy Anderson. Charges alleged the crimes were committed over a period of five months beginning in October of 1945.

He was released on bond, and the charges were held over to the next grand jury. Since the arrest occurred four months before his death, it's likely he hadn't yet been indicted when he died. After his release, Ralph left Juneau to work on a Sitka-based fishing scow, basically a flat-bottomed boat, returning home at the beginning of October 1946. He soon headed back to Sitka, about ninety-five miles to the south, telling his wife he preferred to work there.

And in Sitka he stayed, until Clara got a telegram saying Ralph was in trouble again and flew over to bring him back. Their fight and his ensuing death occurred soon after his return to Juneau. The Nov. 8 edition of the *Sitka Sentinel* newspaper listed Clara and Ralph as passengers on an Alaska Coastal Airlines plane headed to Juneau. The same edition – and the same page – contained a two-paragraph story about Clara killing Ralph. The Sentinel was not a daily paper.

At the time of the killing, Clara Andrews was fifty-three, though she told people she was fifty. After Ralph's death was reported, she was charged with second-degree murder. She was jailed in the federal courthouse.

The killing and the charges were covered in depth by Juneau's daily newspaper. It reported that the Andrews had a history of domestic conflicts. So, the immediate picture that came to mind was of them arguing in their home, ending with her throwing the water glass (called a tumbler in court documents) across the room with great force.

But that wasn't what happened, and Ralph's death was not instantaneous, as the headlines had suggested. Reading Dr. Blanton's statement to the court makes it clear that Andrews was not Blanton's favorite patient. The newspaper account of his testimony stated:

"He further testified that Andrews, a known morphine addict, had 'used up all his veins for morphine injections' and that when plasma was ordered after the victim's pulse began to sink rapidly (just as sewing up the injury was being completed), there were no veins into which the life-saving fluid could be injected."

Despite what appears to be callous treatment of the injured man, the doctor faced no repercussions. Blanton was a respected man, a competitive shooter, a member of the bowling league, and an officer in the Territorial Medical Association. He also helped with the local soapbox derby contest.

Although she had been charged with murder, testimony at the initial court hearing showed Clara Andrews acted in self-defense when she struck Ralph and that she had reason to be frightened of him. Court testimony described Ralph drinking throughout the day of his death. He knew Clara had hidden a bottle somewhere in their boarding-house apartment, and Ralph demanded she give it to him. She resisted but eventually gave in.

He asked her to have a drink with him and she did. She then prepared for bed. Ralph finished the bottle and demanded she go out and get another one. An FBI agent, Sid Thompson, told the court she either refused or took no action, as she was already in nightclothes and lying down in bed.

Juneau police officer John Homme, who had responded to the scene, said Ralph was drunk when he assaulted Clara that night. The policeman confirmed she was lying in bed when Ralph attacked her.

The patrolman said Ralph, a tall man weighing about two hundred pounds, beat her on the head, jaw, chest, and legs with a metal trash can during what the newspaper called a quarrel over a bottle of whisky. Homme mentioned finding the can, with dents in it caused by the assault. The glass, on a bedside table, was the first thing Clara could reach to fend him off.

The court also heard testimony from another doctor, John Clements, who had examined Clara twice. He said he found bruises on her legs, upper body and head. Her lower jaw was distended and discolored. When asked, she displayed some of her injuries to the judge.

Three days after being jailed, Clara was released after posting a $14,000 property bond, based mostly on the value of her boarding house. Adjusted for inflation, that sum totaled almost $236,000 in 2025.

Despite the testimony from the police officer and doctor, Prosecutor Boochever continued criminal action against Clara. He took the case to the grand jury, which met once a quarter (every three months) in 1946. The grand jury did not hear the case until late March 1947.

It returned no true bill. That meant there were no charges. Clara Andrews was free. After the front-page banner headlines suggesting her guilt, that action only merited a paragraph on Page 2 of the *Daily Alaska Empire*.

Clara showed up in the newspaper a few times after that. She was listed as a witness at a wedding about three months after charges were dropped. In 1948, an ad in the newspaper announced Clara, a paid-up *Empire* subscriber, had won two movie tickets. The film was *Good News*, a romantic musical about a college football star and a part-time librarian. A taxi ride to and from the theater was included.

Two years later, the delinquent city tax roll list showed her owing $141.20. And the city fined her $50 for keeping improper business records, but no serious offenses were ever recorded against her.

In 1950, Clara left Juneau and resumed using the last name of her first husband, Frederick Effler. That same year, the census shows Clara living in New Jersey, as the head of a household including her elderly parents and younger sister, Theresa, who had never married. Theresa worked as a secretary.

At some point, Clara and Theresa moved to Clearwater, Florida. Clara Marie Berthold Effler died there in January of 1986 at the age of ninety-two. The sisters rest together at Calvary Catholic Cemetery and Mausoleum in Clearwater.

The assistant U.S. attorney who charged her, Robert Boochever, was at the beginning of a very successful legal career. He eventually served as chief justice of the Alaska Supreme Court and as a circuit judge for the United States Court of Appeals.

Chapter 10: Dismemberment in Sitka

If Barbara Rivers hadn't panicked after the death of her husband, Paul, she might have been able to walk away. After all, it was December 1957 in the little coastal Alaska town of Sitka; the days were short, cold, and wet. It had been two days since she had dismembered his body, flushing the toes and fingers (from which she stripped the skin to remove fingerprints) down the toilet and throwing the torso, arms, legs, and head off a wooden bridge into the ocean. Why she remained in the hotel where her husband spent his final days, instead of taking a steamship south, is perhaps the biggest mystery behind this death.

Barbara and Paul had wed in Portland, OR just four months before. At the ages of forty and forty-four respectively, it would appear they had enough life experience to enter into marriage judiciously. While the marriage certificate states that Paul was a widower, it states that Barbara was single. It is likely that she was divorced or widowed, since her last name on the marriage certificate was not her maiden name of Booth but that of Reese. Shortly after the marriage, they moved to Juneau, where Paul worked as a cook and Barbara at a dry cleaner. She was a seamstress, according to the marriage certificate.

She and Paul had come to Sitka from Juneau under assumed names; perhaps trying to leave behind the troubles the couple had in the past. In Sitka, the Black couple would have been conspicuous among a population about evenly divided between Alaska Natives and Whites. Paul was from Virginia, and Barbara was from Tennessee, so it's likely their voices would have been as distinctive as their appearance.

Downtown Sitka in the 1950s.

After arriving in Sitka on Nov. 27, 1957, the Rivers took up residence at the Alaska Hotel, a building which had been relocated near the waterfront after construction began on the Alaska Pioneers Home, intended to be a territorial rest home for indigent elderly Alaska men. It wasn't unusual in Alaska for buildings to be moved rather than torn down. Homes, and occasional businesses, were often built by fishermen, leading to tight construction reminiscent of boats. It was also common practice to have no basements in the marshy land of Southeast Alaska, but instead to place buildings on wooden stumps. As the stumps rotted, buildings were simply jacked up and the stumps replaced.

The Alaska Hotel's new location put it just a block away from downtown Sitka's most famous landmark, St. Nicholas Russian Orthodox Church, which is placed squarely in the middle of Sitka's main street, forcing traffic to pass it on each side. Like most businesses in Sitka, the Alaska Hotel didn't discriminate against non-Whites. It would have been poor business practice to do so in a town that was only 50% White. While some communities in Alaska, including Juneau, Anchorage, and Fairbanks, made a practice of open discrimination, Sitka had been a Native village for long before Whites entered the picture and continued their strong cultural and business traditions.

Even before Paul's death, the Rivers' presence had been noted. A resident of Sitka from the time recalls hearing that before Paul's death, he had been abusive toward Barbara and was apparently insisting she work as many hours as she could while he stayed at the hotel, drinking. Barbara found work at a Sitka dry cleaner, but the couple had not yet found permanent lodging.

Five days after their arrival, Paul went to see a local physician, Dr. Isaack Knoll. Paul told the doctor he suffered from chronic pain and had trouble sleeping. Barbara later said that Dr. Knoll told Paul to stop drinking and smoking. After he left the doctor, she said, Paul began doing both. He also began hitting her, which she said was a frequent occurrence.

That evening, Dr. Knoll paid a house call on the couple at the hotel, leaving them with sleeping pills and morphine. Today, such a doctor's visit would seem remarkable; it was not at the time.

Barbara later described what happened after the physician left. She said she and Paul both took sleeping pills, which were almost certainly barbiturates, and Paul took the morphine given by Dr. Knoll. She said Paul took two sleeping pills and may have taken more. He quickly passed out, lying on their bed. She said that she was afraid he would wake up and continue hitting her. So, she tied his hands to the bedframe and then wrapped a piece of the same cord loosely around his neck, also tying that to the bedframe. She then took a sleeping pill and went to sleep next to her husband.

The combination of morphine and a barbiturate would have slowed his respiration significantly, especially since Paul had also been drinking. Being forced by Barbara's action to sleep lying flat on his back would have prevented a natural reaction to impeded breathing, that of rolling over or trying to sit up. It, perhaps, isn't surprising that Barbara found herself lying next to a dead man in the morning.

What happened next isn't as easy to explain. If Paul died as Barbara described, most wives would have sought medical

An aerial shot of the bridge where Barbara Rivers disposed of parts of her husband. The wooden bridge has since been replaced by a rock driveway. *Courtesy of Sandy and Thad Poulson*

assistance, or at least alerted authorities. Instead, Barbara decided to get rid of the body. Using at least one meat cleaver, she dismembered Paul's body, probably in the hotel room's bathtub, and then used the toilet to get rid of as much of the body as she could. She flushed fingers, toes, his scalp, lips, and nose. She also skinned the fingertips, to remove fingerprints.

What Barbara didn't know was that Sitka had no sewage treatment in 1957; anything flushed from toilets on the waterfront went to pipes that emptied into the ocean. At low tide, the beaches were littered with toilet paper and other flushed debris.

A couple hundred yards from downtown Sitka and directly behind the 1957 location of the Alaska Hotel is a small island that originally housed a fish saltery in the 1800s, when Sitka was the Russian capital of Alaska. Now, the rock foundation of the saltery held up the distinctive private home of the Cushing family, who owned the local telephone company. In 1957, the home was reached by a wooden bridge. (It now has a rock causeway to the house.) Barbara took the rest of the body – its torso, head, and dismembered limbs - to this bridge, less than a block away behind the hotel, and dumped the parts over the bridge's railing. She most likely carried the body parts in cardboard boxes, since plastic bags would have been more difficult to find, and none were apparently found during the ensuing search. She would have had to make several trips to rid herself of all the body parts, but no one saw her.

That is a little surprising; the weather on Dec. 4, 1957 hovered around freezing, and it wasn't raining, which is unusual in Sitka during the winter. But it was pitch dark by 3:30 p.m. in December, there were no lights on the bridge to the house, and few people would have been outside in the cold.

By the end of the day on Dec. 4, all of Paul Rivers' body had been dumped into the Pacific Ocean. But Barbara Rivers, born in Tennessee, did not understand tidal action or currents. In the absence of strong winds, the protected water in Sitka Sound washed almost all the pieces of Paul's body onto the shore, where they joined the smaller pieces flushed down the toilet at the Alaska Hotel. The largest part of the body – the torso – floated into the wooden bridge to the Cushing house and stayed there, caught by the pilings. If anyone had bothered to look, Paul's torso, legs, and arms would have been readily visible.

But no one was looking. His absence was apparently not noticed by anyone. Perhaps stuck in Sitka due to fear, lack of funds, or a combination of both, Barbara Rivers was left at the Alaska Hotel, now alone and waiting for something to happen. It is possible that, from her window at the hotel, she could see the torso of Paul's body caught up in the bridge.

It is difficult to understand the level of fear and trepidation she may have felt. It is likely there were few people in Sitka with whom she would have felt an affinity. The 1950 census counted thirty-five Black people in Sitka's population of three-thousand. The town itself in the 1950s was a pretty closed community – composed of fishermen, small business owners, and employees at the large hospital operated by the Indian Health Service. A Japanese-owned pulp mill, which would become the town's economic engine for more than two decades, was just starting construction.

As a victim of domestic violence, it is possible that Barbara was feeling lost and aimless after Paul's death. Her decision to rid herself of his physical presence would not have removed the lasting impact of his abuse, which likely created a sense of helplessness. She was a Black woman from the South with no friends or family within thousands of miles. She was in a small, isolated community with an inexperienced police force. She would have expected to be immediately arrested if found with the body of her husband, regardless of the circumstances of his death.

So, she waited. She waited for someone to notice Paul was missing. Perhaps she, alone among all Sitkans, had recognized she was seeing dismembered limbs among the rocks and dark sand of the beach.

On Dec. 5, the day after she woke up to a dead husband and disposed of his body, she could wait no longer. It was late – around 11:00 p.m., when the police received an anonymous phone call from a woman who said Paul Rivers was missing.

And again, Barbara's lack of local knowledge betrayed her. In 1957, phone calls in Sitka were placed through an operator. Calls to the police were routinely sent to wherever in town the operator knew the on-duty police officer was. On this night, the patrolman, Paul Potts, was at the Pioneer Café, about five blocks from the Alaska Hotel. He would have informed the operator of his location before leaving the station, so he took the call at the café. The woman told him a man named Paul Rivers had been murdered, dismembered and his body thrown from the bridge behind the

The bridge as it appeared on a snowy winter day. *Courtesy of Sandy and Thad Poulson*

Alaska Hotel. When asked her name, she said she could be killed if she revealed what she knew.

Of course, the operator knew where the phone call came from – the Alaska Hotel. So, a woman with a southern accent calls the police to say that a Black man named Paul Rivers is missing, and the call came from the hotel where the man and his wife have a room.

Within twenty minutes of receiving the call, police had found the body's torso, lying on the rocks under the bridge to the Cushing house. Half an hour later, police found Mrs. Rivers in front of the Alaska Hotel and asked her if she had made a phone call to the police. She said no. The men continued searching the beaches and found the head, calves, feet, and a forearm with a hand, but no fingers. All these body parts were scattered in an area that stretched about one hundred feet along the beach.

At about 3:00 a.m. on Friday morning, Deputy Federal Marshal Chuck Johnstone and three police officers, including Potts, knocked on Mrs. Rivers' door at the Alaska Hotel. They asked for permission to search the room, which she gave. She told them she hadn't seen her husband in two days. They didn't find anything of note in the room.

There were subsequent searches for the remaining pieces of the body, conducted by Marshal Johnstone and police. Within a day, they had found everything but one arm, from elbow to shoulder. In addition to the marshal and police officers looking, they also relied on volunteers, including boys, according to the newspaper, and continued looking for other evidence. A daughter of the Cushings, who owned the house on the island, entertained her classmates with her grisly story of finding a toe on the beach.

On Dec. 7, four days after the death, searchers found what police referred to as "the second cleaver" that had been used by Barbara to dismember her husband's body. It was found on the beach, a few hundred yards from the body parts. She apparently walked further from the hotel to dispose of the cleaver. There is no further mention of any other cleaver in news accounts or court records.

Meanwhile, police continued to speak with Barbara Rivers. A territorial police officer (as opposed to city police) talked to her again on Dec. 6, the day after the police were called. That interview occurred in the late afternoon, and the officer, Ed Dankworth, recognized her from where she worked at the dry cleaner in Juneau. At the time, Dankworth was based in Juneau; he must have come to Sitka to investigate the Rivers' killing.

Barbara told Dankworth that she hadn't seen Paul since the morning of Dec. 4, when he asked her to purchase wine for him and she refused. She said he dressed and left the hotel room, and she hadn't seen him since.

She also told Dankworth that she wanted to see Paul's remains; he told her they were being examined by Dr. Michael Bierne. Two days later, about 2:00 a.m. on Dec. 8, Dr. Bierne finished his examination. He and Dankworth then went to the federal marshal's meeting to discuss the findings. Dankworth asked if Mrs. Rivers could be brought to the meeting, and she was. Dr. Bierne said his findings were not definitive as to proving Rivers' identity, but he believed he was, based on what Mrs. Rivers had said about his appearance. Dankworth then told Barbara that Dr. Bierne also believed that she killed her husband. She said she did not.

Dankworth then said Mrs. Rivers confessed to having tied the cord around her husband's neck and admitted to making the call to the police and to dismembering the body and throwing it into the ocean. At Dankworth's request, Barbara signed a statement describing the doctor's visit and a fight afterward, during which Paul threw her on the bed. In the statement, she said that after he fell asleep, she "had boiled up inside," which led to her tying his hands to the bed and tying the cord around his neck. She said she then took a sleeping pill and went to sleep. She said that the last words her husband spoke to her were, "you dirty bitch."

After confessing to the police, Barbara was quickly indicted by the Sitka grand jury, which met just a week after she had called police. At this proceeding, she was represented by Sitka attorney Warren Christiansen, one of a small handful of lawyers practicing in Sitka. He had little or no experience with murder charges.

As she waited for the grand jury to meet and then to be taken to Juneau for the ensuing trial, Barbara Rivers was kept in the jail on the third floor of the territorial building, which now houses Sitka city offices. With a woman in the jail, officials needed to bring in a woman warden, and chose Alice Johnstone, wife of Sitka Marshal Chuck Johnstone. Mrs. Johnstone vividly recalls both Barbara and the case.

"She was a scared woman. She was a Black woman in a White town," said Mrs. Johnstone. She said she recalled hearing that Barbara had "accidentally killed her husband." She had also heard that Barbara's husband drank and beat her. In jail, Mrs. Johnstone said that Barbara would cry at night, saying, "I didn't mean to kill him."

Another longtime Sitkan, Nurse Dorothy "Brownie" Thomsen said she met Mrs. Rivers while she was staying at Sitka Community Hospital and liked her. "She was nice. Very quiet." Thomsen said she couldn't recall why she was at the hospital but said that Barbara was also hospitalized when she was taken to Juneau at St. Ann's

Hospital. There, the nurses once told Thomsen that Rivers "had deserved to die," alluding to his abusing Barbara.

The Sitka newspaper dedicated a lot of front-page space to covering the preliminary hearings in Sitka when Barbara was charged and wrote a vivid description of Barbara in its Dec. 9 edition.

"Showing little visible emotion but under considerable strain, Mrs. Barbara Rivers, 42, was arraigned before U.S. Commissioner Earl Shennett at 2 p.m. this afternoon on a charge of first-degree murder of his husband, Paul Rivers.

"Wearing a light blue cardigan, beige stag pants and black high heeled pumps, Mrs. Rivers sat with hands clenched while the complaint was read. She is of medium height, attractive and appears far younger than her age."

The speed of the grand jury indictment was matched by the speed of the trial, which occurred less than three months after Paul's death. It was held in Juneau because there wasn't a territorial judge in Sitka. Unfortunately, the Juneau newspaper didn't cover the trial, and the Sitka newspaper didn't have the resources to send a reporter to attend. So, it was up to the Associated Press reporter to follow the short trial, and that reporter also apparently did not attend the trial; his coverage seems to rely solely on conversations he had with participants at the end of each day. Consequently, the coverage was sparse and consisted mostly of wrap-up descriptions of each day's events.

The trial began Monday, Feb. 17, 1958, with jury selection, about ten weeks after the death. Defense attorney Warren Christiansen now had another lawyer on his team, Albert White. The prosecutor in the case was U.S. District Attorney Roger G. Connor. The addition of Albert White may be another indication of Christiansen's lack of experience. White was best known as a controversial leader in Alaska's Republican Party. He had served as its general counsel for many years, and in 1960, the local newspaper called him an attorney specializing in the real estate

Barbara Rivers Not Crazy Says Gov't. Witness

Dr. John Riley testifies she denies slaying her husband

Churchill ill

NICE, France ⑭ Sir Winston Churchill, 83, remained in bed at his Riviera vacation villa today after what was described as a slight chill. His secretary said he

Council holds line on new appraisals

Headline stating that Barbara Rivers is not crazy, from the Daily Sitka Sentinel, Feb. 19, 1958.

business. He appears to have been as inexperienced in a murder defense as was his co-counsel.

District Attorney Connor, a Navy veteran, had a more illustrious legal career than either White or Christiansen. He had been appointed by President Truman to serve as District Attorney for the First Judicial District (Southeast Alaska) in May 1956 and served in his position for only three years before going into private practice. In 1968, he was named to the Alaska Supreme Court and served there until 1983.

In 1958, he was a relatively new prosecutor but was facing two inexperienced defense attorneys, a solid (and sordid) case, and a friendly judge.

In his opening statement, Barbara's main attorney, Warren Christiansen, brought up the history of Paul's abuse of Barbara, a theme he continued raising throughout the short trial.

The prosecutor focused on the graphic nature of the dismemberment, showing a series of photos to jurors depicting the body parts as they were found. Christiansen objected to the photos, pointing out that dismembering a body was not against the law, but the judge allowed them. The prosecutor also brought in a fingerprint expert who identified the victim as Paul Rivers based on the fingerprint fragments found (which would have again emphasized the dismemberment). On day two of the trial, District Attorney Connor introduced a psychiatrist who declared that Barbara Rivers was not insane.

Defense attorney White may have scored some points under cross-examination, when the psychiatrist stated Barbara said she had not killed her husband and did not recall cutting up the body.

On day three of the trial testimony, Barbara took the stand to tell the jury the same thing – she had no recollection of dismembering the body. She again recounted her decision to tie a loose cord around Paul's neck before she fell asleep.

The next day, the judge provided his instructions to the jury as the trial ended. Jury instructions can play a vital role in deliberations. The judge is seen as an impartial arbiter, so their directives are usually relied upon heavily by jurors.

In this case, Judge Raymond Kelly may not have been as impartial as would be desired. Like others at the time, he appears to have had definite ideas on the issue of domestic violence. Just a year after Paul River's death, Kelly presided over another domestic assault case in Sitka, involving another Black couple. His actions in that case were illustrative of his attitudes.

In 1957, a fifty-eight-year-old man named Arthur Tebo had taken a job in Sitka as a rock breaker with a road construction crew. He was a tough character – he had served time for murder and been arrested for both gambling and assault. Now in Sitka, he was surprised to find that his girlfriend, who he thought was living in Petersburg, was in Sitka, and in a relationship with another man.

Helen Hayden, thirty-eight, had met Tebo in Ketchikan, and they had a relationship. She said his possessiveness frightened her; he had threatened to kill her if she saw anyone else. Eventually, she convinced him to help her buy a restaurant in Petersburg. He gave her $1,500 for it. But instead of moving to Petersburg, she moved to Sitka in hopes of escaping Tebo. Once there, she contacted Sitka police and reported her concerns about Tebo. This was later confirmed in testimony from police.

Now Tebo was in Sitka and heard that Helen was seeing another man, George Hughes, who was known by Tebo. Tebo went to Hughes's home and found the couple in bed. He pulled a gun, and the two men struggled for it. Helen Hayden put a coat on over her nightgown and ran to a nearby cafe to call the police.

Hughes gave up the struggle and ran from the house, chased by Tebo, now carrying a shotgun. Police arrived and went to the hotel where Tebo was staying. There, they found a gun hidden in a shoe. He was arrested for assault. When the case went before Judge Kelly, he decided the real blame for the assault lay with Helen Hayden. In his sentencing Tebo to two years of a suspended sentence, Judge Kelly wrote:

"There seems little doubt that he (Tebo) showed marked jealousy toward the woman in this case; he went so far as to threaten her life, but this was more a matter of words than deeds; when he had an opportunity to shoot her when he found her in bed with another man (as he asserts), he made no aggressive move toward her. Certainly, she was largely at fault in the entire matter; she took the defendant's money quite willingly; she caused him considerable financial losses and deceived him about her going to Sitka instead of to Petersburg to take care of the restaurant business defendant had set up for her. Both this defendant and George Hughes are now sadder and wiser men...."

In the Rivers trial, defense attorney Warren Christiansen made his best attempt to persuade this same judge to give the jury instructions that would be more sympathetic to Barbara Rivers. He did not succeed.

Judge Kelly, in fact, told the jury that any claim of Paul Rivers having abused his wife were not to be considered in their deliberations. He wrote:

"The doctrine of self-defense may be invoked by one who, having been assaulted by another, reasonably believes himself to be in imminent danger of death or of receiving great bodily harm, and who uses whatever force is necessary to prevent such harm.

"You are instructed that in the present case the facts are not such as to make the doctrine of self-defense applicable, and therefore you are not to consider that doctrine in determining the guilt or innocence of the defendant."

He did agree with Christiansen that dismembering a body was not a criminal offense, but also said it could be considered by the jury:

"The dismemberment of the body may be considered by you as bearing upon the question of malice, intent, and in connection with the possible consciousness of guilt, but the defendant is not charged here with any crime in connection with the act of dismembering the body."

Perhaps what is most surprising about the trial and defense is the lack of an effort by the defense attorneys to question the cause of death. Dr. Bornstein, who had performed the autopsy, determined the cause of death to be strangulation. He appeared to base that decision on Barbara's confession of tying the cord about Paul's neck, since his autopsy was concluded in one day and didn't note any evidence of blood tests to check for the presence of alcohol or drugs in the body. Given that the head was removed from the torso, it's unclear how he decided that Paul Rivers had been strangled, unless he based it solely on Barbara's confession of tying him.

Barbara stated that Paul had been drinking throughout the day before he took both morphine and barbiturate-based sleeping pills. That alone could have killed him, and Barbara's decision to tie him in such a way as to prevent his turning on his side or lifting his head would have contributed to decreased respiration.

So what about the doctor who gave him the medication? Dr. Isaack Knoll had been practicing in Sitka for about thirteen years by the time he arrived for the hotel room house call. He had started in practice with another doctor but moved his practice several times during his years in Sitka. Surprisingly, so far as newspaper coverage of Barbara's trial would indicate, he was not called as a witness. He could have confirmed Paul's drinking and threats to Barbara.

Brownie Thomsen, a Sitka nurse who was the administrator of Sitka's first community hospital, built in 1956, remembers Dr. Knoll having a poor reputation. She said she remembered him as having bad sanitation practices and not being well liked. That reputation was reflected in a petition signed by 350 Sitkans after he was appointed to the position of health officer by city officials the year after Paul Rivers' death. The petition opposed the appointment and asked for another physician to be named. Knoll resigned at the council meeting where the petition was presented, referring to a "whispering campaign" against him. He left Sitka the following year without any official notice that he was closing his practice.

Dr. Knoll disappeared into the veils of history once he left Sitka; ensuing articles in the Sitka newspaper suggest he had gone into practice elsewhere; first in Brooklyn, NY and then in Cleveland, Ohio, but there is no hard evidence he worked in either location.

Knoll's decision to leave strong medications with a man who had been drinking certainly calls his judgment into question. Nurse Thomsen said such an action would have been considered unusual, even in 1957. Most physicians of the time would not have been so quick to give potentially deadly medication to a patient they barely knew.

Given the judge's jury instructions, it's not surprising that after six hours of deliberations, the jury voted to convict Barbara Rivers of first-degree murder. Judge Kelly stood ready to impose sentence. Immediately after the jury declared its verdict, he sentenced Barbara to life at hard labor. It is likely that Barbara may have benefited from the Territorial Legislature's decision in 1957 to abolish the death penalty.

In studying historic murder cases in Alaska during territorial days, this case is a rarity in the severity of the sentence. Whether a federal prison could even impose a sentence of hard labor is a question, and it's certain that Barbara Rivers did not actually experience the hard labor portion of her sentence. Instead, she began serving her time at San Pedro Penitentiary in California, a location that earned the moniker Club Fed at one point in its history. Barbara was housed at San Pedro until 1977, when all the women in the co-ed facility were transferred elsewhere due to overcrowding. It has remained a male-only penitentiary in the years since.

It's unknown where Barbara Rivers served the remainder of her sentence or what happened at the end of her life; the federal archives do not have records for several of the inmates from federal facilities prior to 1982. She does not appear in records after that date.

Paul Rivers is buried in the Sitka city cemetery.

Afterword: While Barbara Rivers disappeared into the shroud of time and lack of federal inmate records, some of the people who played a role in her story did not. Ed Dankworth, the territorial police officer who got her confession, went on to lead the Alaska State Troopers before becoming a well-known (and controversial) legislative member and then lobbyist for oil companies. Brownie Thomsen, after serving as administrator for Sitka Community Hospital, took a job as office nurse to a new doctor in Sitka, in 1967. My dad, George Longenbaugh, came to Sitka with his wife and three children, including me, in 1963 as a surgeon with the public health service. He loved Sitka and went into private practice there in 1967 with Brownie as his office nurse. In 2024, when we were researching this story, Brownie is still alive and remembered Dr. Knoll and Barbara Rivers.

Alice Johnstone, the wife of the federal marshal in Sitka, Chuck Johnstone, remained in Sitka for decades after she listened to Barbara Rivers cry in the Sitka jail. She and her husband are well known for their years of efforts to protect and preserve Alaska's old growth national forest. She was living in California at the time of writing.

Acknowledgments

This book is the second I've written on historic murders in Alaska prior to statehood in 1959. As with the first book, I've chosen stories that have more than just a beginning. They are also stories that tell us about a place and time in five communities here in Southeast Alaska.

I continue to rely upon my husband, Ed Schoenfeld, a well-known noted reporter and editor who covered Southeast news for forty-five years. His attention to detail, steady presence, patience, and willingness to look at hours of microfilm have made the past forty years better in every way. Our daughters, Maggie and Elizabeth Schoenfeld, continue to offer support, love and a seemingly endless willingness to hear stories about murder.

Branching out to other communities has been its own challenge – learning about the territorial days of Ketchikan, Tenakee Springs, Sitka, and Petersburg. I have again relied upon the kindness of strangers (who are no longer), especially Vicki Wisenbaugh of Tenakee Springs, Dave Kiffer of Ketchikan, and Brownie Thomsen of Sitka. My aunt and uncle, Sandy and Thad Poulson, also generously loaned me the photo of their Sitka home, which was once the Cushing house, whose bridge was used by Barbara Rivers for disposing of her husband's body.

Patient friends proofread and edited the manuscript, especially Anitra Waldo and Elizabeth Bagley, as well as Ed Schoenfeld. Again, I relied upon the staff at the Alaska State Historic Library and Archives for their assistance in digging through records and guiding our research.

Finally, I want to recognize the impact these crimes had on the people who were victims, their friends and family members, and the killers themselves, who sometimes appear to have chosen their deadly paths through fear, accident, or just plain bad judgment. I hope these stories bring to life those whose lives were ended so abruptly and violently.

AUTHOR BIOGRAPHY

Betsy Longenbaugh is a lifelong Alaskan who was raised in Sitka, AK, and has lived in Douglas, AK, for more than 40 years. She began her professional life with a journalism degree as a newspaper reporter in Sitka and Juneau, and ended it with a master's in social work, working as a social worker for the U.S. Coast Guard. She and her husband, newspaper and radio reporter and editor Ed Schoenfeld, raised two daughters in Douglas and have now replaced going to work every day with walking the dog every day. Betsy and Ed have conducted murder story walking tours in Juneau for the Juneau-Douglas City Museum since 2018, and have presented on the topic at several venues. She is the author of "Forgotten Murders from Alaska's Capital" and the novel, "Death in the Underworld," both published by Epicenter Press.

www.ingramcontent.com/pod-product-compliance
Lightning Source LLC
Chambersburg PA
CBHW011734020426
42333CB00024B/2889